TUSCANY AND FLORENCE
TRAVEL GUIDE
2024-2025

A guide to explore, Rolling green hills, charming villages, ancient buildings, stunning architecture, world-class museums, Outdoor Activities and local experiences

JANE M. BEASLEY

Copyright © 2024 by Jane M. Beasley

All rights reserved. No part of this book may be reproduced, distributed, or transmitted in any form or by any means, including photocopying, recording, or other electronic or mechanical methods, without the prior written permission of the publisher, except in the case of brief quotations embodied in critical reviews and specific other noncommercial uses permitted by copyright law

TABLE OF CONTENTS

INTRODUCTION..7
   Overview of the Region..9
   Why Tuscany and Florence?......................................10
   How to Use This Guide...12
CHAPTER 1...14
PLANNING YOUR TRIP..14
   When to visit Tuscany and Florence..........................14
   Duration of your trip...18
   Tuscany and Florence on a budget...........................20
   Choosing the right tour package...............................23
   Entry and visa requirements.....................................27
CHAPTER 2...30
GETTING TO TUSCANY AND FLORENCE........................30
   Choosing the Best flights..30
   Tuscany and Florence airport: Arrival and Orientation.....34
   Journey to Tuscany and Florence..............................37
   Train Options..39
   Bus Options..42
   Any other travel option for Tuscany and Florence......44
   Navigating Tuscany: Car, Train, and Public Transport.....46
CHAPTER 3...48
FLORENCE: THE CRADLE OF RENAISSANCE................48
   Introduction to Florence..48
   Essential Florence Sights..50
   Hidden Gems of Florence...52
   Food and Wine in Florence: Local Cuisine and Famous Restaurants..54
   Shopping in Florence: From Leather to Artisanal Goods. 56

CHAPTER 4...59
THE ART AND ARCHITECTURE IN FLORENCE................59
    Renaissance Masterpieces... 59
    Churches, Basilicas, and Monasteries.............................. 61
    Public Art and Monuments.. 63
    Florence's Gardens and Green Spaces........................... 66

CHAPTER 5...69
TUSCAN CITIES BEYOND FLORENCE............................ 69
    Pisa: The Leaning Tower and Beyond............................. 69
    Siena: The Palio and Gothic Splendor.............................72
    Lucca: Medieval Walls and Charming Streets................75
    Arezzo: Art, Antiques, and History................................... 78
    Livorno: The Port City with a Character......................... 81
    Pistoia: Off-the-Beaten-Path Discovery...........................84

CHAPTER 6...87
THE TUSCAN COUNTRYSIDE.. 87
    Chianti: Rolling Hills, Vineyards, and Wineries................ 87
    Val d'Orcia: Scenic Drives and Picture-Perfect Landscapes 91
    Maremma: Tuscany's Wild Coastline................................ 94
    Casentino: Forests, Castles, and Sacred Sites................97
    The Hilltop Towns of Tuscany: San Gimignano, Volterra, and Montepulciano.. 100

CHAPTER U7... 103
TUSCANY' WINE REGION... 103
    Introduction to Tuscan Wines... 103
    Chianti Classico: The Heart of Tuscan Wine.................106
    Montalcino: Home of Brunello....................................... 108
    Montepulciano: Vino Nobile... 110

Bolgheri: The Super Tuscans...................................... 112
CHAPTER 8...**115**
FOOD CULTURE IN TUSCANY....................................**115**
    Traditional Tuscan Dishes.. 115
    Olive Oil: The Liquid Gold of Tuscany....................... 118
    Tuscan Markets: Fresh Produce and Local Delicacies.. 124
CHAPTER 9...**126**
EXPERIENCING THE TUSCAN LIFESTYLE....................**126**
    Cultural Etiquette and Language Tips........................ 126
    Agriturismos: Staying on Tuscan Farms..................... 128
    Slow Living and Slow Food Movement....................... 130
    Festivals and Traditions.. 132
    Artisanal Crafts: Pottery, Leatherwork, and Textiles....... 133
    Sustainable Travel: Eco-Friendly Options.................... 135
CHAPTER 10...**137**
OUTDOOR ACTIVITIES..**137**
    Hiking Trails and Nature Reserves.............................137
    Biking Through the Vineyards and Countryside........... 140
    Hot Springs and Spas.. 143
    The Tuscan Archipelago: Islands of Elba and Giglio...... 146
CHAPTER 11...**149**
DAY TRIPS FROM FLORENCE......................................**149**
    Fiesole: Ancient History and Spectacular Views............ 149
    Vinci: The Birthplace of Leonardo.............................. 151
    Prato: Textiles and Contemporary Art......................... 153
CHAPTER 12...**155**
TUSCANY FOR FAMILY..**155**
    Kid-Friendly Attractions... 155
    Best Activities for Families: Castles, Farms, and Parks. 158

    Planning a Family Itinerary in Tuscany 161
CHAPTER 13 165
PRACTICAL INFORMATION 165
    Money matters and Currency Exchange 165
    Language and Communication 169
    Emergency Contacts 173
    Useful Websites and Apps 176
CONCLUSION 179
    MAP 182

INTRODUCTION

Tuscany and Florence are like scenes from a dream. Imagine rolling green hills, charming villages with ancient buildings, and a culture rich in history and art. Florence, the heart of Tuscany, is famous for its stunning architecture, world-class museums, and vibrant street life. The Tuscan countryside is dotted with vineyards and olive groves, offering a peaceful escape from the bustle of city life.

My own journey to Tuscany began with a simple TikTok challenge—recreating famous scenes from Tuscan films. What started as a fun idea quickly turned into a passionate exploration of this beautiful region. I was drawn to Tuscany's captivating landscapes and rich cultural heritage. When I arrived, the reality surpassed even my wildest expectations.

In Florence, I roamed the cobblestone streets, stood in awe before the grand Duomo, and explored the Uffizi Gallery, home to masterpieces by Michelangelo and Botticelli. I ventured into the Chianti region, savoring the renowned wines, and trekked through the Cinque Terre, where the coastal views were nothing short of spectacular.

But the real magic came from the small, unexpected moments. I learned to make carbonara from a local pasta shop owner, found a quiet beach for serene swims, and discovered a quaint bookstore with a rare first edition of Dante's Divine Comedy. These personal experiences made my trip unforgettable.

In this book, you'll find more than just a guide to Tuscany and Florence. You'll discover the hidden gems and personal adventures that make this region truly special. From detailed advice on must-see sights to insider tips on where to find the best local experiences, this guide is designed to help you explore Tuscany and Florence like a seasoned traveler. So, if you're dreaming of a journey that blends history, beauty, and unforgettable moments, dive into these pages and let Tuscany and Florence enchant you just as they did me.

Overview of the Region

Tuscany and Florence are two of Italy's most captivating destinations. Tuscany is a region in central Italy known for its stunning landscapes, charming towns, and rich cultural history. Imagine rolling hills covered in vineyards and olive groves, medieval villages with narrow streets, and picturesque countryside views. It's a place that feels like stepping into a beautiful painting.

Florence, the capital of Tuscany, is often described as the cradle of the Renaissance. It's a city full of art, history, and stunning architecture. Florence is home to famous landmarks like the Florence Cathedral with its impressive dome, the Uffizi Gallery which houses masterpieces by artists like Leonardo da Vinci and Botticelli, and the Ponte Vecchio, a historic bridge lined with shops.

When you visit Tuscany, you'll find a mix of experiences that make it unique. The countryside is dotted with charming towns like Siena, known for its medieval architecture and the famous Palio horse race, and San Gimignano, famous for its medieval towers and beautiful views. The region is also renowned for its wine, especially in areas like Chianti, where you can visit vineyards and enjoy wine tastings.

Florence offers an urban experience with its rich museums, lively piazzas, and excellent dining options. The city's historic center is a UNESCO World Heritage Site, and wandering through its streets feels like exploring a living museum. From the art-filled corridors of the Uffizi to the bustling markets where you can sample local delicacies, Florence is a city where history and modern life blend seamlessly.

Tuscany and Florence together provide a complete Italian experience. Whether you're exploring ancient towns, enjoying world-class art, or relaxing with a glass of Chianti, you'll find that this region has something to offer every traveler. It's a place where every corner has a story to tell, and every moment can become a cherished memory.

Why Tuscany and Florence?

Tuscany and Florence are exceptional destinations that capture the essence of Italy's charm and beauty. Tuscany, with its lush landscapes and historic towns, offers a picturesque escape from the everyday. The rolling hills, dotted with vineyards and olive groves, create a serene setting that's perfect for relaxation and exploration. This region is not just about its beautiful scenery, but also about its rich cultural heritage. From ancient Etruscan ruins to medieval castles, Tuscany is steeped in history that invites you to delve into its past.

Florence, the heart of Tuscany, is a city where history comes alive. It is renowned for its remarkable contributions to art and culture during the Renaissance. Walking through Florence feels like stepping back in time, as you encounter masterpieces by artists like Michelangelo and Leonardo da Vinci. The city's architecture is a marvel, with the iconic Florence Cathedral and its impressive dome standing out as a symbol of artistic achievement. Florence's museums, such as the Uffizi Gallery and the Galleria dell'Accademia, showcase some of the most important works of art in the world.

The combination of Tuscany's countryside and Florence's urban vibrancy makes this region uniquely appealing. Tuscany offers a tranquil retreat with its charming villages, scenic vineyards, and delicious local cuisine. You can enjoy leisurely strolls through quaint towns, taste exceptional wines, and savor traditional dishes that highlight the region's agricultural richness.

Florence, on the other hand, provides a dynamic cultural experience. It's a city where you can immerse yourself in art, history, and lively street life. From exploring Renaissance art to dining in cozy trattorias, Florence blends historical significance with contemporary energy.

Choosing Tuscany and Florence means experiencing the best of both worlds: the peaceful beauty of the countryside and the cultural richness of a historic city. Whether you're drawn to the art and history of Florence or the scenic beauty and local flavors of Tuscany, this region promises an unforgettable journey full of discovery and delight.

How to Use This Guide

This guide is designed to help you make the most of your visit to Tuscany and Florence. It's packed with practical information, insider tips, and personal recommendations to ensure you have a fantastic experience.

Start by exploring the sections that interest you most. If you're eager to dive into Florence's art scene, look for detailed descriptions of must-see museums and galleries. You'll find helpful tips on what to see and do, along with suggestions for where to eat and stay nearby.

For those planning to explore the Tuscan countryside, there's plenty of advice on charming villages, scenic drives, and local wineries. Whether you want to hike through picturesque landscapes or sample delicious local wines, you'll find guidance on the best spots to visit and activities to enjoy.

The guide also includes practical tips on how to get around. It covers transportation options like renting a car or using public transit, so you can easily navigate between Florence and the surrounding areas. You'll also find advice on the best times to visit, so you can plan your trip to avoid crowds and make the most of your time.

Throughout the guide, you'll discover personal insights and experiences that add a unique touch. These recommendations aim to help you find hidden gems and special moments that might not be in the typical tourist brochures. Whether it's a cozy café with the best coffee or a lesser-known viewpoint with breathtaking views, these tips are designed to enhance your travel experience.

By using this guide, you'll have a comprehensive resource to help you plan and enjoy every aspect of your trip to Tuscany and Florence. From historical landmarks to local favorites, it will provide you with the information you need to create lasting memories and make the most of your adventure.

CHAPTER 1.
PLANNING YOUR TRIP

When to visit Tuscany and Florence

Spring in Tuscany and Florence

Spring in Tuscany and Florence is a time of renewal and vibrant colors. From March to May, the region shakes off winter's chill, and the landscape comes alive with blossoming flowers and lush greenery. The weather is pleasantly mild, with temperatures ranging from 10°C to 20°C (50°F to 68°F), making it an ideal time for outdoor activities. The rolling hills of Tuscany are covered in wildflowers, and the countryside is at its most picturesque. In Florence, the pleasant weather is perfect for strolling through its historic streets and gardens.

Practical tips for spring travel include packing layers to accommodate the fluctuating temperatures. A light jacket and comfortable walking shoes are essential. Rain showers are occasional, so bringing an umbrella or raincoat is wise.

Spring offers numerous activities and events. In Florence, the Easter festivities are particularly notable, with vibrant processions and celebrations. The countryside hosts various festivals, such as the Infiorata flower festival, where towns decorate their streets with elaborate flower carpets. Booking accommodations and tours in advance is recommended, as spring is a popular time for visitors.

Crowds start to build up in spring, particularly around Easter, but they are still manageable compared to the summer months. Prices for flights and accommodations may begin to rise, so early booking can help secure better rates. Compared to summer's heat and crowded attractions, spring offers a more relaxed and comfortable experience.

Summer in Tuscany and Florence
Summer in Tuscany and Florence, from June to August, is a season of warmth and bustling activity. Temperatures can soar to 30°C to 35°C (86°F to 95°F) in Tuscany, and Florence can be quite hot, with highs reaching 40°C (104°F). The landscape is golden and dry, with vineyards and fields ready for harvest. It's a lively time, with outdoor events, festivals, and bustling markets.

Pack light, breathable clothing, sunscreen, and a hat to protect yourself from the sun. Comfortable walking shoes are essential for exploring, and a refillable water bottle will keep you hydrated.

Summer is a great time for experiencing Tuscany's wine harvest festivals and outdoor concerts. Florence hosts various cultural events, including open-air operas and performances in historical venues. However, the summer months can be very hot, especially in the cities, and reservations for accommodations and popular attractions are essential due to high demand.

The summer season sees the highest number of tourists, leading to crowded attractions and higher prices for flights and accommodations. To avoid the peak heat and crowds, consider visiting in early June or late August. Booking well in advance can help manage costs and secure your preferred options.

Autumn in Tuscany and Florence
Autumn, from September to November, brings a beautiful transformation to Tuscany and Florence. The weather is cooler and more comfortable, with temperatures ranging from 15°C to 25°C (59°F to 77°F). The landscape is painted with rich hues of red, orange, and gold as the leaves change color. Harvest season is in full swing, and the vineyards and orchards are abundant with fresh produce.

When traveling in autumn, pack layers for cooler mornings and warmer afternoons. A light jacket and comfortable walking shoes are suitable, and don't forget a scarf for the crisp evenings.

Autumn is ideal for experiencing the harvest festivals and truffle hunts that Tuscany is known for. Florence offers a more relaxed pace compared to summer, with fewer tourists but plenty of cultural activities. The Chianti wine harvest festivals are a highlight, with local wine tastings and traditional foods. Make reservations for truffle tours and wine tastings in advance, as these experiences are popular during the harvest season.

Crowds are smaller compared to summer, and prices for flights and accommodations are generally lower. Autumn offers a pleasant balance between good weather and fewer tourists, making it a wonderful time for both sightseeing and enjoying local festivals.

Winter in Tuscany and Florence
Winter, from December to February, brings a serene and quieter atmosphere to Tuscany and Florence. Temperatures

range from 0°C to 10°C (32°F to 50°F), and while snow is rare in the cities, it can dust the countryside and mountains. The region's landscapes are tranquil and beautiful, with fewer tourists around, offering a more intimate experience.

Pack warm clothing, including a coat, gloves, and scarves, to stay comfortable during cooler days. It's also a good idea to bring layers for indoor heating and outdoor exploration.

Winter is a special time for experiencing holiday festivities, including Christmas markets and New Year's celebrations. Florence's Christmas lights and holiday markets are a delight, and Tuscany's small towns host charming local celebrations. This season is perfect for enjoying the local cuisine, with hearty dishes and warm wines. However, some attractions may have reduced hours or be closed, so checking in advance is advisable.

Winter sees the fewest tourists and the lowest prices for accommodations and flights. This is a great time to visit if you prefer a quieter experience and don't mind cooler weather. Compared to the bustling summer months, winter offers a peaceful and reflective atmosphere, making it an appealing choice for a more relaxed getaway.

Tuscany and Florence offer unique experiences throughout the year, each season bringing its own charm and opportunities. Whether you're looking for vibrant festivals, serene landscapes, or cultural immersion, you can find the perfect time to visit based on your interests and travel goals.

Duration of your trip

Deciding how long to spend in Tuscany and Florence depends on what you want to experience and how much time you have available. Here's a guide to help you plan the duration of your trip.

For a short visit of about three to four days, you can enjoy a taste of both Florence and Tuscany. In Florence, focus on the main attractions like the Florence Cathedral, the Uffizi Gallery, and the Ponte Vecchio. You can also take a leisurely stroll through the city's charming streets and enjoy some local cuisine. With this limited time, consider taking a half-day or day trip to a nearby Tuscan town such as Pisa or Siena to get a glimpse of the countryside.

If you have a week, you can explore Florence more thoroughly and have enough time to venture into Tuscany. Spend a few days in Florence visiting its museums, historic sites, and enjoying its vibrant street life. Then, allocate a few days to explore the Tuscan countryside. You might visit charming towns like San Gimignano or Montepulciano, go wine tasting in Chianti, and take in the beautiful landscapes. A week gives you a nice balance between city life and countryside relaxation.

For a more in-depth experience, a ten-day to two-week trip allows you to fully immerse yourself in both Florence and Tuscany. You can spend several days in Florence, exploring its lesser-known neighborhoods, art galleries, and enjoying the local cuisine at a leisurely pace. In Tuscany, you can visit a range of towns and regions, taking your time to explore each one. You might also include more activities like cooking classes, guided tours, and longer excursions into the countryside. This extended stay lets you appreciate the rich culture, history, and beauty of the region without feeling rushed.

The duration of your trip should match your interests and how deeply you want to explore Tuscany and Florence. A short visit is perfect for a quick introduction, while a longer stay allows for a more comprehensive experience. No matter how long you stay, you'll find plenty to see and do in this captivating region.

Tuscany and Florence on a budget

Exploring Tuscany and Florence on a budget can be a rewarding experience, allowing you to enjoy the region's beauty and culture without overspending. Here's a comprehensive guide to help you make the most of your trip affordably while maintaining comfort and enjoyment.

Timing Your Visit
To maximize your budget savings, consider visiting Tuscany and Florence during the shoulder seasons, which are typically from mid-March to May and from September to October. During these months, you can enjoy pleasant weather and fewer tourists compared to the peak summer season. Prices for accommodations and flights are generally lower, and you'll find that popular attractions are less crowded, making for a more relaxed experience. The off-season, from November to February, also offers significant savings, although the weather can be cooler and less predictable. However, the lower prices for flights and accommodations can offset the chill.

Accommodation Options
Finding budget-friendly lodging in Tuscany and Florence is quite feasible with a bit of research. Hostels and guesthouses offer affordable rates and a chance to meet fellow travelers. For instance, in Florence, you might consider staying at Hostel Gallo d'Oro, where beds can be as low as 25-35 euros per night, depending on the season. In Tuscany, look into agriturismos (farm stays), which often provide a charming experience at a reasonable price. For example, Agriturismo La Palazzina near Siena offers rooms starting around 60 euros per night. Vacation rentals can also be a good option;

platforms like Airbnb have many budget-friendly choices, with prices starting from about 50 euros per night for a private room or apartment. To find the best deals, book early and consider staying slightly outside the city center to save on accommodation costs.

Activity Planning
You can enjoy Tuscany and Florence's key attractions without breaking the bank. Many of Florence's museums and galleries offer discounted or free entry on certain days of the month. For example, the Uffizi Gallery often has free entry on the first Sunday of each month. In Tuscany, explore the numerous free attractions such as the charming towns of San Gimignano and Volterra, where wandering through the streets and enjoying the local architecture comes at no cost. Many cities also host local festivals, markets, and events that are free or low-cost. In Florence, the Piazza della Signoria and the Ponte Vecchio are iconic landmarks that you can enjoy without spending a cent. Consider free walking tours, which are often tip-based, offering a great way to learn about the city's history and culture.

Dining on a Budget
Dining affordably in Tuscany and Florence is quite manageable with a bit of planning. Look for local trattorias and osterias where you can enjoy authentic Italian meals at lower prices. In Florence, places like All'Antico Vinaio are famous for their delicious and reasonably priced panini. In Tuscany, small local markets and bakeries often offer fresh, affordable food options. For a unique experience, consider picnicking in one of Florence's many beautiful parks, such as

the Cascine Park or the Boboli Gardens. You can purchase fresh produce, cheeses, and bread from local markets to create a delightful meal. Additionally, street food is a fantastic way to sample local flavors without overspending. Try the famous Florentine street food, lampredotto, which is both delicious and budget-friendly.

Transportation and Additional Tips
When it comes to getting around, use public transportation to save money. Florence has a well-connected bus system, and many attractions are within walking distance of each other. For exploring Tuscany, consider regional trains and buses, which are generally affordable and offer a chance to see the countryside. Purchasing a Firenze Card or similar city pass can offer savings on public transportation and admission fees to multiple attractions. To get the most out of your budget-friendly visit, also keep an eye out for special offers and discounts, such as city tours and museum passes that might offer savings if booked in advance.

Experiencing Tuscany and Florence on a budget is entirely possible with thoughtful planning. By timing your visit wisely, choosing affordable accommodations, planning activities strategically, and finding cost-effective dining options, you can enjoy all the beauty and culture these destinations have to offer without spending a fortune. Remember, memorable experiences often come from the simple pleasures and local interactions, not lavish spending.

Choosing the right tour package

Selecting the best tour packages for Tuscany and Florence can transform your trip from a simple getaway into an unforgettable adventure. Here's a comprehensive guide to help you navigate the various options and find the tour package that best suits your needs and interests.

Types of Tour Packages
Tuscany and Florence offer a range of tour packages catering to different preferences. Guided tours are a popular choice, providing an enriching experience with a knowledgeable guide who shares insights into the region's history, art, and culture. These tours often include visits to major attractions like the Uffizi Gallery and the Duomo, and sometimes offer behind-the-scenes access. For instance, a typical full-day guided tour might cost between 70 to 150 euros per person, depending on the inclusions.

Self-guided walking tours are another option, ideal for travelers who prefer exploring at their own pace. These packages often come with detailed maps, audio guides, or apps that offer information about key sights and local tips. This option is generally more affordable, with prices ranging from 20 to 60 euros, and allows for a flexible itinerary.

Adventure excursions are perfect for those seeking more active experiences. These can include activities such as wine-tasting bike tours through Chianti, hot air balloon rides over the Tuscan countryside, or hiking excursions in the scenic hills. Prices for these adventure tours vary widely, with options ranging from 80 to 200 euros or more, depending on the length and type of activity.

Detailed Information
When choosing a tour package, consider the duration, cost, and inclusions. For example, a classic Florence city tour might last around four hours, costing about 80 euros and including entry fees to major sites and a guided walk through historic neighborhoods. In contrast, a full-day Tuscan countryside tour might last 8 to 10 hours, costing between 120 to 200 euros, and could include transportation, lunch, and wine tastings.

Tour packages that include meals, transportation, and entry fees can provide great value, especially if you prefer a more all-inclusive experience. Check what is covered in each package—some might include skip-the-line access to popular attractions, which can save you time and enhance your visit.

Traveler Suitability
Different tours cater to various types of travelers. Families might enjoy guided tours that are both educational and entertaining, with family-friendly activities and amenities. For example, a day tour that combines visits to historic sites with interactive experiences, such as cooking classes, can be ideal for families with children.

Couples may prefer romantic tours, such as private wine tastings or sunset walks through Florence. Packages that include scenic views, intimate dining experiences, and opportunities for leisurely exploration can make for a memorable trip.

Solo adventurers can benefit from self-guided tours, which allow them to explore at their own pace and discover hidden gems. Small-group tours can also offer a social aspect while still providing the flexibility of guided exploration.

Groups might look for customized or private tours that cater to their specific interests, such as art-focused tours or multi-day excursions covering different regions of Tuscany.

Seasonal Considerations
The availability and experience of tour packages can vary with the seasons. During peak tourist seasons, such as summer, tours might be more crowded and prices higher. It's advisable to book in advance to secure your spot. Spring and autumn are ideal times for touring, as the weather is pleasant and the crowds are smaller. Winter tours can be quieter and offer a chance to experience Tuscany and Florence with fewer tourists, though some tours might be limited or less frequent during this period.

Local Insights
Local guides and previous travelers often provide valuable insights into the best tour experiences. Look for tours that include off-the-beaten-path destinations or lesser-known attractions. For example, exploring the Etruscan ruins in Volterra or enjoying a wine-tasting tour in lesser-known vineyards can offer unique experiences beyond the typical tourist spots.

Booking Tips

To book a tour package, research reputable tour operators and read reviews from past travelers. Look for operators with good ratings and transparent information about what's included. Booking directly through local tour operators can sometimes offer better rates than third-party booking sites. Always check for any hidden fees and confirm the cancellation policy before finalizing your booking.

Personalization and Flexibility
Many tour packages offer customization options to fit personal preferences. You can often combine different tours or add special experiences to create a tailored itinerary. For example, you might choose a guided city tour in Florence and then add a day trip to the Tuscan countryside. Contact tour operators to discuss your interests and see if they can adjust the package to better suit your needs.

Choosing the right tour package involves balancing your interests, budget, and travel goals. By understanding the types of tours available, considering the best times to visit, and researching thoroughly, you can ensure a memorable and enjoyable experience in Tuscany and Florence. With thoughtful planning, you can make the most of your trip and create lasting memories.

Entry and visa requirements

When planning a trip to Tuscany and Florence, understanding entry and visa requirements is crucial for a smooth travel experience. Here's a detailed guide to help you navigate these requirements effectively.

Visa Requirements

To determine if you need a visa for Italy, including Tuscany and Florence, start by checking your nationality against Italy's entry requirements. Most travelers from countries within the European Union (EU) or Schengen Area do not need a visa for short stays. The Schengen visa is the primary visa for non-EU travelers, allowing them to visit Italy and other Schengen countries for up to 90 days within a 180-day period.

Countries typically covered under the Schengen visa include the United States, Canada, Australia, and several other countries outside the EU. To check if you need a visa, visit the official Schengen visa information website or the Italian embassy website relevant to your country.

Visa Application Process

1. Determine Visa Type: For most travelers, the Schengen visa is required. Ensure you apply for this visa if you're traveling from a non-EU country that does not have a visa-free agreement with Italy.

2. Prepare Required Documents: Gather all necessary documents for your visa application:
    - Passport: Valid for at least three months beyond your intended departure date from the Schengen Area. Ensure it has at least two blank pages.

- Travel Itinerary: Proof of travel arrangements, including flight bookings.
- Accommodation Bookings: Confirmation of where you will be staying in Tuscany and Florence.
- Proof of Financial Means: Evidence that you have sufficient funds to cover your stay, such as bank statements or a letter from your employer.
- Travel Insurance: Coverage for medical emergencies during your stay.

3. Complete Visa Application Form: Fill out the Schengen visa application form. This can often be completed online or downloaded from the consulate's website.

4. Schedule an Appointment: Book an appointment with the nearest Italian consulate or embassy to submit your application. Some countries also offer visa application centers (VACs) that handle submissions.

5. Submit Application and Pay Fees: Attend your appointment with all required documents and pay the visa application fee. Fees can vary depending on your nationality and the type of visa.

6. Attend an Interview: Depending on your country of origin, you might need to attend an interview at the consulate. Be prepared to discuss your travel plans and provide any additional information requested.

7. Wait for Processing: Visa processing times can vary, so apply well in advance of your travel dates. Typically, processing takes about 15 calendar days but can be longer during peak seasons.

8. Receive Your Visa: Once approved, you will receive your visa stamped in your passport. Check all details for accuracy.

For official resources and to confirm the latest visa requirements, visit the Schengen visa website or the Italian embassy's website in your country.

Practical Tips
Start the visa application process early to avoid last-minute issues. Use official resources to ensure you have the most current and accurate information. Double-check that all documents are complete and correctly formatted.

Interactive Elements
To help with the process, consider creating or using interactive tools such as a checklist of required documents or a flowchart outlining the steps for visa application. These tools can simplify the process and ensure you don't miss any crucial steps.

For instance, a U.S. citizen planning a two-week vacation in Tuscany and Florence would need to apply for a Schengen visa, following the steps outlined above. They would submit their application with proof of travel arrangements, accommodation in Italy, and adequate travel insurance.

Conversely, a Canadian traveling for the same duration might have a similar process but should confirm any specific requirements through the Canadian visa application center or the Italian consulate.

By following these steps and tips, you can ensure a smooth visa application process and focus on enjoying your trip to Tuscany and Florence.

CHAPTER 2.
GETTING TO TUSCANY AND FLORENCE

Choosing the Best flights

When planning a trip to Tuscany and Florence, selecting the best flights can make a significant difference in both comfort and cost. Here's a comprehensive guide to help you navigate your options and find the ideal flight for your journey.

Major Airlines and Routes

Several major airlines offer flights to Tuscany and Florence or nearby airports. For direct flights to Florence, you can fly with airlines such as Delta Air Lines, which provides seasonal service from major U.S. hubs like New York and Atlanta. American Airlines and United Airlines also offer routes to Florence, although these flights are often seasonal and may require connections.

If you're flying from locations where direct flights aren't available, you might consider flying into nearby airports like Pisa or Bologna. Pisa International Airport, about an hour's drive from Florence, is served by airlines like Ryanair, EasyJet, and Alitalia, offering numerous connections from various European cities. Bologna Guglielmo Marconi Airport, around an hour and a half away from Florence, also has flights operated by major European carriers such as Lufthansa, Air France, and British Airways.

Flight durations from the U.S. to Florence typically range from 9 to 11 hours for direct flights, with potential layovers extending travel time. European flights usually take about 2 to 3 hours, depending on your departure city.

Finding the Best Deals
To secure the best flight deals, start by booking your tickets well in advance. Prices tend to be lower when booked several months before your departure date. Flexibility with your travel dates can also help you find better fares. Use price comparison websites like Skyscanner or Google Flights to compare prices across different airlines and booking platforms.

Setting fare alerts on these websites allows you to monitor price changes and grab a good deal when it appears. Keep an eye out for airline sales and promotions, which often occur during off-peak seasons or specific times of the year.

Seasonal Variations
Flight prices and availability can fluctuate based on the season. High season for Tuscany and Florence is typically during the summer months (June to August) when the weather is warm and tourist activity is at its peak. During this time, flights can be more expensive and harder to secure. Shoulder seasons, like late spring (April to May) and early autumn (September to October), often offer more reasonable prices and fewer crowds. Winter months (November to March) usually have the lowest prices, although some attractions and services may have reduced hours or availability.

Airport Fees and Taxes

When flying into Tuscany and Florence, be aware of potential airport fees and taxes. These can vary depending on the airline and departure location. In Europe, airport taxes are often included in the ticket price, but additional fees might apply for services such as extra baggage or priority boarding. To minimize these costs, check the airline's fee structure before booking and avoid optional extras if possible.

Baggage Policies
Baggage policies can vary significantly between airlines. For major international airlines, economy class typically includes one carry-on bag and one checked bag. However, budget airlines like Ryanair or EasyJet may charge additional fees for checked luggage and limit the size of carry-ons. Be sure to review the baggage allowance for your chosen airline and plan accordingly. If you have oversized or additional luggage, check the airline's policy on fees and pre-purchase baggage options to save money.

Travel Classes and Amenities
Airlines offer several travel classes, each with its own set of amenities. Economy class is the most budget-friendly option, while premium economy provides extra space and comfort for a higher price. Business class offers superior comfort, priority boarding, and access to lounges, and first class provides the highest level of luxury and service. If you're looking for additional comfort but are on a budget, premium economy might be a good compromise. For longer flights, the amenities in business or first class can enhance your overall experience.

Booking Tips

When booking your flight, aim for mid-week travel as flights are often cheaper than on weekends. Navigate airline websites carefully, and always read the cancellation policies and check for travel insurance options. Insurance can provide peace of mind in case of unforeseen changes to your travel plans.

Loyalty Programs
If you frequently travel, consider joining an airline loyalty program. These programs offer rewards such as points or miles that can be redeemed for flights, upgrades, or other perks. Frequent flyers can benefit from priority boarding, additional baggage allowances, and access to lounges. Check if your chosen airline is part of an alliance like Star Alliance or SkyTeam, which can provide additional benefits when flying with partner airlines.

By carefully considering these factors and planning accordingly, you can choose the best flights that fit your needs and preferences, ensuring a comfortable and enjoyable journey to Tuscany and Florence.

Tuscany and Florence airport: Arrival and Orientation

When you arrive in Tuscany and Florence, navigating the airport and getting oriented is a key step to starting your adventure smoothly. Here's a detailed guide to help you through the arrival process and get acquainted with your surroundings.

Arrival at the Airport

If you're flying directly into Florence, you'll land at Amerigo Vespucci Airport, also known as Florence Airport. It's a small airport but well-equipped to handle international and domestic flights. Upon arrival, you'll go through passport control and customs. The airport staff is generally helpful, so don't hesitate to ask for assistance if you need it.

After clearing customs, you'll find yourself in the baggage claim area. If you have checked luggage, retrieve your bags from the designated carousel. For those with only carry-on luggage, you can head directly to the arrivals hall. Here, you'll find a range of services including currency exchange, car rental desks, and information counters.

If you're flying into Pisa or Bologna, you'll need to take additional steps to reach Florence. Pisa International Airport is about an hour's drive from Florence. You can take a direct train from Pisa to Florence's main train station, Santa Maria Novella. Alternatively, there are shuttle buses that run regularly between the airports and Florence.

Bologna Guglielmo Marconi Airport is slightly farther, about an hour and a half by car. From Bologna, you can take a train to Florence, which usually takes about 35 to 50 minutes. There are also bus services that connect Bologna to Florence.

Getting Around and Orientation
Once you're at the airport, you'll need to decide how to get to your accommodation. If you're in Florence, taxis are readily available outside the airport. You can also use rideshare apps like Uber or Lyft, which operate in Florence. For those who prefer public transportation, the airport is connected to the city center by a direct tram line. The tram stop is conveniently located near the airport terminal.

If you're arriving at Pisa or Bologna, you can use train services to reach Florence. The train stations at Pisa and Bologna are well-connected and offer frequent services to Florence. For convenience, check the schedules and buy tickets in advance if possible. Trains are a comfortable and scenic way to travel through Tuscany.

Airport Facilities
Florence Airport has a variety of facilities to make your arrival comfortable. There are cafes and shops where you can grab a bite to eat or buy travel essentials. Free Wi-Fi is available throughout the airport, so you can easily connect and plan your next steps. If you need to freshen up or wait for a pickup, there are seating areas and restrooms available.

Pisa and Bologna airports also offer similar amenities, with shops, dining options, and facilities for travelers. Pisa's airport is slightly larger, offering a broader range of services, including car rental and travel information counters. Bologna's airport, while smaller, is efficient and well-organized.

Getting Your Bearings
As you start your journey in Florence or Tuscany, familiarize yourself with the local transportation options. Florence's city center is compact and easy to navigate on foot, but public buses and trams can also be useful. The main train station, Santa Maria Novella, is centrally located and serves as a hub for both local and regional travel.

In Tuscany, if you plan to explore beyond Florence, renting a car might be a good option. The region is known for its picturesque countryside and charming towns that are best explored by car. Many car rental agencies are available at the airports, and it's advisable to book in advance to secure the best rates.

Orientation Tips
To help with orientation, pick up a local map or download a navigation app on your smartphone. Many cities in Tuscany, including Florence, have tourist information centers where you can get maps, brochures, and advice on local attractions.

Starting your trip with a clear understanding of the airport procedures and local transportation will set the stage for a smooth and enjoyable experience in Tuscany and Florence. Whether you're heading to the heart of Florence or exploring the Tuscan countryside, this guide will help you navigate your arrival with ease and confidence.

Journey to Tuscany and Florence

When embarking on a journey to Tuscany and Florence, the experience starts the moment you begin planning your trip. Here's a straightforward guide to help you make your way to this enchanting region smoothly and enjoyably.

The journey to Tuscany and Florence can start from various points around the world. If you're flying, your options will largely depend on where you're coming from. Florence has its own airport, Amerigo Vespucci Airport, which is a convenient entry point if you're traveling directly to the city. For many travelers, however, arriving at larger international airports like Pisa International or Bologna Guglielmo Marconi is common.

From Pisa, the trip to Florence is about an hour by train. The Pisa Airport train station is well-connected to the city, making it a straightforward journey. You can also take a direct shuttle bus from Pisa to Florence, which can be a bit more comfortable if you have a lot of luggage or prefer not to navigate train changes. In both cases, it's a good idea to check train or bus schedules in advance and consider purchasing tickets ahead of time to save time and avoid any last-minute stress.

If you arrive in Bologna, the journey to Florence will take approximately 35 to 50 minutes by train. The train service is frequent and reliable, so you can enjoy the scenic route through the Italian countryside. Buses are another option, though they might take a bit longer. Whether you choose a train or a bus, planning your departure times and purchasing tickets in advance can help you manage your travel smoothly.

Upon arrival at Florence's airport or train station, you will be greeted with various transportation options to reach your final destination. If you're staying in Florence, taxis are readily available outside the airport and train station. You can also use rideshare apps, which are quite popular in the city. For a more local experience, the tram line connects the airport to the city center, providing a convenient and efficient means of transport.

When traveling to other parts of Tuscany, renting a car can be highly beneficial. Tuscany is renowned for its picturesque landscapes, rolling hills, and charming towns, which are best explored at your own pace. Car rental services are available at airports and train stations. Booking your car in advance can help secure a better rate and ensure availability.

Once you've arrived in Tuscany, you'll find that getting around is relatively easy. Florence's city center is compact and walkable, with many attractions within a short distance of each other. Public buses and trams are also available for longer distances or if you prefer not to walk. In the broader Tuscan region, driving allows you to visit delightful small towns, vineyards, and historic sites that are scattered across the countryside.

Whether you're traveling directly to Florence or making your way through Tuscany, the journey offers a glimpse of Italy's beauty and charm. The landscapes change as you travel, from the urban vibrancy of Florence to the serene countryside of Tuscany. Enjoy the transition as you move from the city's bustling streets to the tranquil rolling hills of the region.

This journey is the first step in your adventure through Tuscany and Florence. Planning ahead, understanding your transportation options, and embracing the scenic travel routes will help you start your trip on the right foot. With every mile you travel, you'll be getting closer to experiencing the rich history, culture, and beauty of Tuscany and Florence.

Train Options

Traveling by train to and within Tuscany and Florence is a convenient and enjoyable way to experience Italy's beautiful landscapes. Here's a detailed look at your train options for getting around and making the most of your journey.

When you arrive in Italy, you'll find that trains are a popular choice for both long-distance travel and local connections. The Italian train system is well-organized, and trains are generally reliable and comfortable.

If you're flying into Florence, you'll land at Amerigo Vespucci Airport. From there, you can take a taxi, a bus, or a tram to the Florence train station, which is called Firenze Santa Maria Novella. This station is the main hub in Florence and connects you to numerous destinations both within Tuscany and across Italy.

For travelers arriving at Pisa International Airport, the journey to Florence is straightforward. You can catch a train directly from Pisa Airport to Florence. The train station at Pisa Airport is just a short walk from the terminal. Trains from Pisa to Florence run frequently, and the trip usually takes about an hour. This is a convenient and scenic way to start your Tuscan adventure.

If you're traveling from other major Italian cities, such as Rome or Milan, you'll find high-speed trains connecting you to Florence. The high-speed trains, known as Frecciarossa or Italo, offer a fast and comfortable journey. For instance, a train ride from Rome to Florence takes around 1.5 hours, and from Milan, it takes about 2 hours. These trains are modern, with comfortable seating and amenities like free Wi-Fi on some routes.

Once in Florence, the train station serves as a great starting point for exploring the region. Tuscany's beautiful towns and countryside are easily accessible by train. For example, you can take a train from Florence to Pisa, Siena, or Lucca. The train ride to Siena offers a picturesque view of the Tuscan countryside, taking about 1.5 hours. Trains to Pisa also provide a lovely view of the landscape and are a quick trip from Florence.

In addition to regional trains, there are local trains known as "Regionale" that connect smaller towns and cities within Tuscany. These trains are generally slower but are a great way to see the region's charming towns. Tickets for these trains are usually quite affordable.

When planning your train journey, it's a good idea to book tickets in advance, especially if you're traveling on high-speed trains or during peak travel times. Booking ahead can also help you secure better prices. You can purchase tickets online through websites like Trenitalia or Italo, or buy them at the train station.

For a more relaxed and scenic travel experience, consider taking regional trains. They often make stops at smaller towns and offer a glimpse into local life. You can also use the train journey to plan day trips to various Tuscan towns.

Traveling by train in Tuscany and Florence is both efficient and enjoyable. The train network is extensive and well-connected, allowing you to easily explore the region and appreciate its scenic beauty. Whether you're heading straight to Florence or planning to explore other parts of Tuscany, the train options available provide a convenient and pleasant way to get around.

Bus Options

Using buses in Tuscany and Florence is a practical and often cost-effective way to get around and explore the region. Buses offer a range of services, from local city routes to regional connections, making them a great option for travelers looking to experience Tuscany's charming towns and landscapes.

In Florence, the public bus network is operated by ATAF, which provides comprehensive coverage of the city and its suburbs. Buses are a good choice for getting around Florence, especially if you want to visit areas that are not easily accessible by foot or tram. The city buses are frequent and cover major sights, including the Florence Cathedral, Uffizi Gallery, and the Ponte Vecchio. Tickets can be purchased at newsstands, tobacco shops, or on the ATAF app. Make sure to validate your ticket before boarding the bus to avoid fines.

For traveling beyond Florence, you can use regional buses to explore other parts of Tuscany. These buses are operated by various companies, such as the regional bus service, Tiemme, which covers a wide range of destinations within Tuscany. Tiemme buses connect Florence with nearby towns like Siena, Arezzo, and Pisa. The journeys are generally comfortable and offer a scenic view of the Tuscan countryside. Tickets for regional buses can be bought at bus stations, online, or directly from the driver.

If you're planning to visit smaller towns and villages in Tuscany, regional buses are often your best option. These buses may not run as frequently as those in larger cities, so it's a good idea to check schedules ahead of time. Some of the smaller towns, such as San Gimignano or Volterra, are well-served by regional buses, but you might need to transfer at a larger hub, like Florence or Siena.

Traveling by bus is also a budget-friendly way to get around. It is usually cheaper than taking the train, especially for shorter trips or when traveling on regional routes. Be sure to check for any special fares or discounts that might be available for tourists or groups.

For the most convenient travel experience, plan your bus trips in advance. Look up schedules and routes online to make sure you understand how to reach your destinations and what times the buses run. Also, consider purchasing tickets ahead of time if possible, especially during busy travel periods. Many bus companies have websites where you can check schedules and purchase tickets.

Buses offer a flexible and economical way to explore Tuscany and Florence. They are ideal for reaching both popular destinations and hidden gems in the region. With a bit of planning, you can use the bus system to enhance your travel experience and enjoy the beautiful landscapes and cultural sites of Tuscany.

Any other travel option for Tuscany and Florence

In addition to trains and buses, there are several other travel options to consider for getting around Tuscany and Florence, each offering a unique way to experience the region.

One popular option is renting a car. Having your own vehicle provides the freedom to explore Tuscany at your own pace. The region's scenic countryside, vineyards, and charming villages are often best reached by car. Renting a car allows you to visit less accessible places, such as the rolling hills of Chianti or the medieval town of San Gimignano. Be sure to familiarize yourself with local driving regulations and parking rules. In Florence, parking can be challenging and expensive, so it might be better to park outside the city center and use public transport to get into town.

For a more leisurely experience, consider renting a bike. Florence and many towns in Tuscany are bike-friendly, and cycling allows you to enjoy the beautiful landscapes at a relaxed pace. There are various bike rental shops in Florence and other towns, offering everything from city bikes to mountain bikes. This is a great way to explore the city's historic sites or to venture out into the countryside and discover scenic routes.

If you're looking for a more scenic and unique way to travel, hot air balloon rides are available in Tuscany. These rides offer breathtaking views of the Tuscan landscape, including vineyards, olive groves, and charming villages. They are typically operated early in the morning to catch the best light and provide a memorable experience, though they can be on the pricier side.

For those interested in boat travel, especially along the Tuscan coast, there are opportunities for excursions and boat tours. The coastal towns of Tuscany, such as Viareggio and Livorno, offer boat trips that allow you to explore the beautiful Mediterranean coastline, enjoy some time on the water, or even visit nearby islands.

Consider guided tours or day trips offered by various tour companies. These can range from organized bus tours to private excursions. Guided tours are convenient and can be a good way to see multiple destinations in a short amount of time, especially if you prefer not to drive yourself or navigate public transport.

Each of these options offers a different way to explore Tuscany and Florence, allowing you to tailor your travel experience based on your preferences, budget, and desired level of adventure.

Navigating Tuscany: Car, Train, and Public Transport

Navigating Tuscany can be a delightful experience, offering various options to suit your preferences and needs. Here's a straightforward guide to help you get around using cars, trains, and public transport.

Traveling by car is one of the most flexible ways to explore Tuscany. The region's picturesque countryside and charming villages are often best reached by driving yourself. With a rental car, you can easily visit places like the rolling hills of Chianti, the historic town of Siena, or the medieval towers of San Gimignano. It's a great way to experience the freedom of traveling at your own pace. However, be prepared for narrow roads and winding routes, especially in rural areas. In Florence, parking can be a challenge due to limited space and high costs, so consider parking outside the city and using local transport to get in.

Trains are another excellent option, particularly for traveling between major cities and towns. The Italian train system is efficient and connects Florence to other key locations like Pisa, Lucca, and Rome. The main train station in Florence is Santa Maria Novella, centrally located and well-connected. Trains in Tuscany are generally comfortable and offer scenic views of the landscape. It's a good idea to book your tickets in advance, especially during peak travel times, and check the schedule to ensure you're traveling at a convenient time. Regional trains are a bit slower but are ideal for short trips within Tuscany.

Public transport in Tuscany includes buses that serve both urban and rural areas. In Florence, buses cover a wide network, making it easy to reach different parts of the city. The local transport company, ATAF, operates most of the bus services, and tickets can be purchased at kiosks, newsstands, or via mobile apps. For traveling between smaller towns and the countryside, regional buses are available but may have less frequent service compared to trains. It's important to check the bus schedules and routes in advance to ensure you can plan your trips effectively.

Each of these options provides a different way to experience Tuscany, so consider your itinerary and preferences when choosing how to get around. Whether you opt for the flexibility of driving, the convenience of trains, or the accessibility of public buses, navigating Tuscany can be a smooth and enjoyable part of your journey.

CHAPTER 3.
FLORENCE: THE CRADLE OF RENAISSANCE

Introduction to Florence

Florence, the heart of Tuscany, is a city that feels like stepping into a living history book. Nestled in the Arno River valley, it's renowned for its stunning architecture, world-class art, and rich cultural heritage.

As you wander through Florence, you'll be captivated by its breathtaking skyline, dominated by the iconic dome of the Cathedral of Santa Maria del Fiore, often just referred to as the Duomo. This architectural marvel is a testament to the city's medieval past and a symbol of its artistic and architectural prowess. The narrow, cobblestone streets of the historic center are lined with buildings that date back centuries, offering a glimpse into the city's vibrant history.

Florence is known for its art and museums. The Uffizi Gallery is one of the most famous art museums in the world, housing masterpieces by Botticelli, Michelangelo, and Leonardo da Vinci. Nearby, the Accademia Gallery is home to Michelangelo's David, a must-see for anyone interested in Renaissance art. Every corner of Florence is rich with artistic legacy, from its grand palaces and churches to the charming squares and public fountains.

The city also boasts a lively market scene. The San Lorenzo Market, with its bustling stalls, offers everything from fresh produce to leather goods. Here, you can sample local delicacies like Florentine steak and gelato, or pick up souvenirs to remember your visit.

Florence's atmosphere is a blend of the old and the new. While the city is steeped in historical significance, it's also a modern hub with trendy boutiques, cozy cafes, and vibrant nightlife. Whether you're exploring its famous landmarks, savoring traditional Tuscan cuisine, or simply enjoying a leisurely stroll along the Arno River, Florence has a unique charm that makes it a memorable destination.

For anyone planning a trip, Florence offers an experience that combines historical grandeur with contemporary vibrancy, making it a must-visit city in Tuscany.

Essential Florence Sights

Florence is filled with incredible sights that bring its rich history and art to life. Start your visit with the Cathedral of Santa Maria del Fiore, commonly known as the Duomo. This magnificent cathedral is famous for its striking red dome, designed by Filippo Brunelleschi. You can climb to the top for a breathtaking view of the city and the surrounding Tuscan landscape.

Just next to the Duomo is the Baptistery of St. John, an octagonal building known for its beautiful bronze doors, which are often called the "Gates of Paradise." The intricate designs on these doors are a must-see and offer a glimpse into medieval art.

The Uffizi Gallery is another highlight of Florence. It's one of the most important art museums in the world, showcasing masterpieces from the Renaissance period. You'll find works by Botticelli, including "The Birth of Venus," and many other iconic pieces that capture the essence of Renaissance art.

Nearby, the Accademia Gallery houses Michelangelo's "David," a statue that's become a symbol of human achievement and artistic perfection. Seeing this sculpture up close is a powerful experience that brings Michelangelo's craftsmanship to life.

Piazza della Signoria is a lively square where you can see the imposing Palazzo Vecchio, the city's medieval town hall. The square is also home to several impressive statues, including a copy of "David" and the Fountain of Neptune. It's a great place to soak in the atmosphere and watch the world go by.

Crossing the Ponte Vecchio, Florence's most famous bridge, you'll encounter a bustling scene of jewelry shops and beautiful views of the Arno River. The bridge has a rich history and was once home to butchers and other tradespeople before becoming a center for goldsmiths.

For a more serene experience, visit the Boboli Gardens behind the Pitti Palace. These expansive gardens offer a peaceful retreat with well-manicured lawns, fountains, and sculptures. They provide a lovely escape from the city's hustle and bustle and offer panoramic views of Florence from various vantage points.

Finally, don't miss out on the Basilica of Santa Croce, which is not only a beautiful church but also the final resting place of some of Italy's most famous figures, including Michelangelo, Galileo, and Machiavelli. The church itself is adorned with stunning frescoes and provides a deep dive into Florence's historical and cultural heritage.

Exploring these essential sights will give you a rich understanding of Florence's historical and artistic legacy while offering plenty of opportunities to experience the city's charm and beauty.

Hidden Gems of Florence

Florence is known for its iconic landmarks, but the city is also home to a number of hidden gems that offer a more intimate and unique experience. One such gem is the Bardini Gardens. Located on a hillside just east of the more famous Boboli Gardens, Bardini Gardens is a tranquil oasis with stunning views of the city. The gardens feature beautifully landscaped areas, a charming walled garden, and a lovely terrace where you can relax and enjoy the scenery.

Another delightful spot is the San Lorenzo Market, which is often overshadowed by Florence's more famous markets. The San Lorenzo Market is a bustling place where you can explore a variety of stalls selling fresh produce, local cheeses, meats, and baked goods. It's a great place to experience the local food culture and pick up some delicious treats or souvenirs.

For a taste of Florence's vibrant local art scene, visit the Santo Spirito neighborhood. This area is less touristy and offers a glimpse into the everyday life of Florentines. The Piazza Santo Spirito, at the heart of the neighborhood, is a lively square surrounded by cafes and shops. The nearby Basilica of Santo Spirito, designed by Brunelleschi, is a lesser-known but beautiful church with a serene atmosphere.

The Museum of San Salvatore al Monte is another hidden treasure. It is housed in a former convent and features a collection of Renaissance art and artifacts. The museum is less crowded than the major art institutions, providing a more relaxed environment to appreciate its exhibits.

If you're a fan of quirky museums, don't miss the Museum of the History of Science. Located in the Palazzo della Specola, this museum showcases scientific instruments from the Renaissance period, including early telescopes and astrolabes. It's a fascinating place that offers insight into the history of science and innovation in Florence.

For a peaceful retreat away from the crowds, head to the Rose Garden, or Giardino delle Rose. This charming park is situated on the hill of Piazzale Michelangelo and offers panoramic views of the city. The garden is filled with beautifully maintained rose beds and sculptures, making it a perfect spot for a leisurely stroll or a quiet moment of reflection.

Lastly, explore the charming neighborhood of San Frediano, known for its authentic Florentine atmosphere. The area is filled with traditional trattorias, artisan shops, and local markets. It's a great place to wander and experience the city as the locals do, away from the more touristy spots.

These hidden gems offer a chance to experience Florence from a different perspective, allowing you to uncover the city's lesser-known but equally enchanting aspects.

Food and Wine in Florence: Local Cuisine and Famous Restaurants

Florence is a city that delights food lovers with its rich culinary traditions and exceptional wine. The local cuisine is a celebration of simple, high-quality ingredients, and the city's dining scene ranges from rustic trattorias to elegant restaurants. Here's a guide to some of the must-try local dishes and famous eateries in Florence.

For an authentic taste of Florence, start with a visit to Trattoria ZaZa. Located at Piazza del Mercato Centrale 26R, this lively trattoria is famous for its hearty Tuscan dishes. The restaurant's specialty is the Florentine steak, or Bistecca alla Fiorentina, a thick, juicy cut of beef grilled to perfection. To get there, head to the central market area and you'll find it right by the bustling Mercato Centrale.

Another gem is Osteria Santo Spirito, found at Piazza Santo Spirito 16R. This cozy eatery offers traditional Tuscan cuisine in a charming setting. Their menu features dishes like ribollita, a comforting Tuscan vegetable soup, and pici cacio e pepe, a simple pasta dish with cheese and pepper. The restaurant is located in the vibrant Santo Spirito neighborhood, making it easy to explore other local spots after your meal.

For those seeking a more refined dining experience, visit La Giostra, located at Borgo Pinti 12R. This restaurant is renowned for its elegant atmosphere and exquisite food. The menu includes a variety of Tuscan classics, such as the delicious pear and pecorino ravioli. La Giostra is in the heart of Florence's historic center, close to the Duomo and other major attractions.

If you're a wine enthusiast, don't miss Enoteca Pinchiorri at Via Ghibellina 87. This Michelin-starred restaurant and wine bar offers an extensive selection of Italian and international wines, paired with gourmet Tuscan dishes. The setting is sophisticated and perfect for a special occasion. It's a short walk from Piazza della Signoria, so it's convenient for exploring the city.

For a more casual experience, head to Mercato Centrale, located at Piazza del Mercato Centrale. This bustling food market features a variety of stalls offering everything from fresh produce to prepared meals. You can sample a range of local dishes, including sandwiches filled with cured meats and cheeses. The market is a great place to immerse yourself in the local food culture and enjoy a meal in a vibrant atmosphere.

Another great spot for wine lovers is Vini e Vecchi Sapori, located at Via dei Macci 111R. This small, family-run restaurant is known for its excellent wine list and traditional Tuscan dishes. It's a bit off the beaten path but well worth the visit for its authentic flavors and warm hospitality.

To navigate to these locations, you can use public transportation or simply walk, as many are centrally located and close to major landmarks. Florence's historic center is compact and pedestrian-friendly, so exploring on foot is often the best way to soak in the city's charm while making your way to these delicious destinations.

In Florence, food and wine are integral to the city's culture, and these recommended spots offer a taste of what makes

Tuscan cuisine so special. Enjoy the culinary journey and savor every bite.

Shopping in Florence: From Leather to Artisanal Goods

Shopping in Florence is a delightful experience, offering everything from high-quality leather goods to unique artisanal creations. The city is known for its rich tradition in craftsmanship and provides a range of shopping options for visitors looking to take home a piece of Florentine culture.

One of the best places to find exquisite leather goods is the San Lorenzo Market, located at Piazza San Lorenzo. This bustling market is known for its wide selection of leather jackets, bags, and accessories. The stalls here are a treasure trove of well-crafted leather items, and you can often find great deals by haggling with the vendors. To get there, head towards the Piazza San Lorenzo, which is situated near the central train station, Santa Maria Novella.

For high-quality leather products, visit Scuola del Cuoio, at Via San Giuseppe 5R. This renowned leather school and workshop not only sells beautiful leather items but also offers a glimpse into the craftsmanship behind them. The store has a range of products including bags, belts, and wallets, all made on-site. It's located close to the Santa Croce Basilica, making it easy to include in a day of sightseeing.

If you're interested in artisanal goods, make your way to Via dei Neri 11R to visit the boutique L'Artigianato. This store features a curated selection of handmade jewelry, pottery, and textiles crafted by local artisans. The shop is in the heart of Florence's historic center, so you can enjoy a stroll through charming streets as you explore.

For unique souvenirs and high-quality Florentine crafts, stop by La Bottega dell'Orafo at Via degli Strozzi 5R. This shop specializes in fine jewelry and watches, offering a range of elegant pieces that reflect Florence's rich tradition in goldsmithing. It's located near the Piazza della Repubblica, making it a convenient stop while exploring the city center.

If you're looking for a more contemporary shopping experience, head to Rinascente at Piazza della Repubblica 1. This upscale department store offers a wide range of fashion, accessories, and home goods. The store is in a prime location right in the center of Florence, and it's a great place to find both international brands and stylish Italian designs.

For those interested in art and antiques, visit the Antichità Giordano at Via dei Panzani 10R. This shop specializes in antique furniture, paintings, and collectibles. The store offers a glimpse into Florence's rich history through its curated selection of vintage items. It's conveniently located near the main shopping streets, making it easy to explore while you're in the city.

To get to these shopping destinations, you can walk if they are within the central area, or use public transport such as buses or trams, which are well-connected to various parts of the city. Florence's historic center is compact and pedestrian-friendly, so exploring on foot is often the best way to enjoy both the shopping and the city's beautiful scenery.

Whether you're looking for luxurious leather goods, artisanal crafts, or stylish fashion, Florence offers a variety of shopping experiences that cater to all tastes. Enjoy discovering the city's unique shops and take home a piece of Florentine craftsmanship.

CHAPTER 4.
THE ART AND ARCHITECTURE IN FLORENCE

Renaissance Masterpieces

Florence, the cradle of the Renaissance, is home to some of the most iconic masterpieces of this transformative artistic period. Walking through the city is like stepping into a living museum, with masterpieces by renowned artists such as Leonardo da Vinci, Michelangelo, and Botticelli waiting to be discovered. Here's a guide to some of the must-see Renaissance masterpieces in Florence, along with practical information on how to find them.

One of the most famous locations for Renaissance art is the Uffizi Gallery, located at Piazzale degli Uffizi 6. This world-renowned museum houses an extensive collection of Renaissance art, including Botticelli's "The Birth of Venus" and Leonardo da Vinci's "Annunciation." The Uffizi is situated in the heart of Florence, near the Ponte Vecchio, making it easy to reach from most central locations. To get there, you can walk from the Piazza della Signoria, where the gallery is just a short stroll away.

Another must-see is the Accademia Gallery, located at Via Ricasoli 58/60. It's home to Michelangelo's iconic statue of David, a masterpiece of Renaissance sculpture. The gallery also showcases other works by Michelangelo and a collection of Renaissance and medieval art. The Accademia is a short walk from the Florence Cathedral, making it easy to combine your visit with a trip to this other historic site.

The Florence Cathedral, or Duomo, at Piazza del Duomo, is another essential stop. While the cathedral itself is an architectural masterpiece, it's also worth visiting to see the artwork within, including Giorgio Vasari's frescoes on the dome. The Duomo is centrally located and is one of Florence's most recognizable landmarks. You can easily reach it by walking from the central train station or other nearby attractions.

For a glimpse of Renaissance art in a more intimate setting, visit the Palazzo Medici Riccardi, located at Via Cavour 1. This historic palace features frescoes by Benozzo Gozzoli, including the famous "Journey of the Magi." The palace is close to the San Lorenzo Market, so it's convenient to include it in a day of exploring the area.

If you're interested in Renaissance art and architecture, don't miss the Basilica of Santa Croce, located at Piazza Santa Croce. This church is not only known for its beautiful Gothic architecture but also for its tombs of famous Renaissance figures such as Michelangelo and Galileo. Inside, you'll find works by artists such as Giotto, whose frescoes are an integral part of the church's decoration. The Basilica is a short walk from the historic center, making it easy to visit alongside other nearby attractions.

To make the most of your visit to these Renaissance masterpieces, consider booking tickets in advance, especially for the Uffizi and Accademia, as they can get very busy. Guided tours are also available and can provide valuable insights into the history and significance of the artworks you'll see.

Exploring these masterpieces will give you a deeper appreciation for the Renaissance and the incredible talent that emerged from Florence during this period. Whether you're admiring Michelangelo's sculptures, Botticelli's paintings, or the architectural marvels of the Duomo, Florence offers a rich tapestry of artistic heritage to enjoy.

Churches, Basilicas, and Monasteries

Florence is a treasure trove of stunning religious buildings, each with its own unique history and architectural beauty. From grand basilicas to serene monasteries, exploring these sites offers a deep dive into the city's rich spiritual and artistic heritage. Here's a guide to some of the must-visit churches, basilicas, and monasteries in Florence, complete with practical information on how to find them.

The Florence Cathedral, also known as the Duomo, is an essential visit. Located at Piazza del Duomo 50122 Florence, this iconic cathedral is renowned for its striking dome designed by Filippo Brunelleschi. The cathedral's interior features beautiful frescoes and intricate details, while the dome offers panoramic views of the city. To get there, you can walk from the central train station or from nearby landmarks such as the Piazza della Signoria.

Next to the Duomo is the Basilica di Santa Maria Novella, located at Piazza Santa Maria Novella 18. This church is known for its beautiful façade and the stunning frescoes by Giotto and Masaccio inside. It's just a short walk from the main train station, Santa Maria Novella, making it very accessible for visitors.

The Basilica di San Lorenzo, found at Piazza San Lorenzo 9, is another important site. This church was designed by Filippo Brunelleschi and houses the Medici Chapels, where many members of the powerful Medici family are buried. The basilica is a short walk from the San Lorenzo Market, making it convenient to visit while exploring the area.

For a more serene experience, visit the Basilica di Santa Croce, located at Piazza Santa Croce 16. This basilica is famous for its Gothic architecture and the tombs of several prominent figures, including Michelangelo and Galileo. The church is centrally located, and you can easily walk there from other attractions in the historic center.

The Certosa di Firenze, located at Via Vecchietti 11, is a historical monastery situated a bit outside the city center. It's known for its tranquil atmosphere and beautiful cloisters. To get there, you can take a short bus ride or drive from the city center, as it's about a 20-minute journey.

The Convento di San Marco, at Piazza San Marco 1, is another noteworthy site. This former monastery now serves as a museum and contains frescoes by Fra Angelico. It's located near the Accademia Gallery, so it's easy to include in a day of sightseeing. You can walk there from the Accademia or take a short bus ride.

For a unique experience, visit the Basilica di San Miniato al Monte, located at Via delle Porte Sante 34. Perched on a hill overlooking the city, this church offers stunning views of Florence and is known for its beautiful mosaic façade and serene ambiance. It's a bit of a walk uphill from the city center, but the views and tranquility make it worthwhile.

These religious sites not only showcase Florence's architectural and artistic achievements but also provide a glimpse into the city's spiritual history. To make the most of your visits, consider checking opening hours in advance and dressing modestly, as many of these sites are active places of worship. Whether you're admiring the grandeur of the Duomo, exploring the intricate details of Santa Maria Novella, or enjoying the peaceful setting of San Miniato al Monte, Florence's churches, basilicas, and monasteries offer unforgettable experiences.

Public Art and Monuments

Florence is adorned with impressive public art and monuments that showcase the city's rich artistic heritage and history. These landmarks are scattered throughout the city, each offering its own unique story and artistic contribution. Here's a guide to some of the most notable public art and monuments you should explore, including practical information on how to find them.

Start with the iconic Statue of David by Michelangelo, located at Piazza della Signoria, 50122 Florence. This masterpiece of Renaissance art is a replica of the original statue that resides in the Accademia Gallery. The statue stands proudly in front of the Palazzo Vecchio and is a focal point of the square. You can easily reach it by walking from other central attractions, such as the Uffizi Gallery or the Ponte Vecchio.

Another must-see is the Fontana del Nettuno, also known as the Fountain of Neptune, situated at Piazza della Signoria. This grand fountain features a striking statue of Neptune, the god of the sea, and was created by the artist Bartolomeo Ammannati. It's located right in the heart of the square, so you can find it while exploring the area around the Palazzo Vecchio and the Loggia dei Lanzi.

The Ponte Vecchio, Florence's famous medieval bridge, is another significant public art piece. Located at Ponte Vecchio, 50125 Florence, this bridge is lined with shops and offers stunning views of the Arno River. It's a short walk from the Uffizi Gallery and easily accessible from various parts of the city center.

In the Piazzale Michelangelo, located at Piazzale Michelangelo, 50125 Florence, you'll find the replica of Michelangelo's David, set against a panoramic view of Florence. This spot offers one of the best views of the city and is a popular location for photos. To get there, you can take a bus or enjoy a scenic walk uphill from the city center.

The Monument to Dante Alighieri, situated at Piazza Santa Croce, 50122 Florence, honors the famous Italian poet. This statue, designed by Enrico Pazzi, stands prominently in front of the Basilica of Santa Croce. It's located in the square, so you can find it while visiting the basilica or exploring the nearby area.

Another notable monument is the Monument to Giovanni dalle Bande Nere, located at Piazza San Lorenzo, 50123 Florence. This statue commemorates the military leader Giovanni de' Medici, known for his heroic deeds. It's near the

San Lorenzo Market, so you can visit it while exploring the bustling market area.

The Loggia dei Lanzi, located at Piazza della Signoria, 50122 Florence, is an open-air sculpture gallery featuring several notable statues, including the Perseus with the Head of Medusa by Benvenuto Cellini and the Rape of the Sabine Women by Giambologna. This spot is right next to the Palazzo Vecchio, making it easy to include in your exploration of the square.

The Basilica of San Lorenzo, found at Piazza San Lorenzo, 50123 Florence, houses the Medici Chapels, which are decorated with elaborate statues and tombs of the Medici family. The church is close to the San Lorenzo Market, so you can visit it while exploring the area.

Florence's public art and monuments are not only visually stunning but also steeped in historical significance. To make the most of your visits, consider exploring these sites on foot or by using the city's convenient public transportation options. Whether you're admiring the grandeur of Michelangelo's David, enjoying the scenic views from Piazzale Michelangelo, or exploring the artistic treasures of Piazza della Signoria, Florence's public art and monuments offer a rich tapestry of cultural experiences.

Florence's Gardens and Green Spaces

Florence is not just about art and architecture; it's also home to stunning gardens and green spaces that offer a peaceful escape from the bustling streets. These gardens are perfect for relaxing, enjoying nature, and taking in the beauty of the Tuscan landscape, all within the city. Here's a guide to some of Florence's most beautiful gardens and green spaces, including how to find them.

The Boboli Gardens are a must-see for anyone visiting Florence. Located at Piazza de' Pitti, 1, 50125 Florence, these Renaissance gardens are part of the Pitti Palace. Spread across 111 acres, the gardens feature beautifully landscaped lawns, sculptures, fountains, and shaded pathways. You can easily spend a few hours wandering through the gardens, soaking in the history and enjoying the panoramic views of the city. To get there, you can walk from the Ponte Vecchio or take a bus to the nearby Pitti Palace.

For a quieter and less touristy experience, head to the Bardini Garden at Costa S. Giorgio, 2, 50125 Florence. This garden offers breathtaking views of Florence and the Arno River. With its terraced layout, beautiful flowers, and elegant statues, Bardini Garden is a peaceful retreat. It's a short walk from the Boboli Gardens, making it easy to combine the two for a full day of exploring Florence's green spaces.

If you're looking for a more intimate space, the Rose Garden is a delightful choice. Located at Viale Giuseppe Poggi, 2, 50125 Florence, this small garden is perched on the hillside below Piazzale Michelangelo. The Rose Garden offers stunning views of the city, and during the spring, it's filled with blooming roses. It's a short walk uphill from the city center, or you can take a bus to Piazzale Michelangelo and walk down.

For families or those seeking a large, open space, the Cascine Park is the perfect spot. Located along the Arno River at Piazzale delle Cascine, 50144 Florence, this is the largest public park in the city. It offers wide walking paths, playgrounds, and plenty of room for picnics. You can rent bikes to explore the park or simply enjoy a relaxing afternoon by the river. To reach Cascine Park, take the tram line from the city center directly to the park's entrance.

The Giardino dell'Orticoltura, located at Via Vittorio Emanuele II, 4, 50139 Florence, is another lovely green space in the city. Known for its large greenhouse and well-maintained gardens, this park is great for a peaceful stroll or a quiet afternoon reading a book. It's a bit outside the main tourist areas, but you can easily reach it by bus from the city center.

Finally, if you're looking for a true hidden gem, visit the Botanical Garden of Florence, known as Giardino dei Semplici, at Via Pier Antonio Micheli, 3, 50121 Florence. Established in 1545, it's one of the oldest botanical gardens in the world. With a wide variety of plants and a calm, academic atmosphere, it's the perfect place to escape the crowds. You can get there by walking from Piazza San Marco or by taking a bus to the nearby stops.

Florence's gardens and green spaces offer a peaceful contrast to the city's historic streets and museums. Whether you're exploring the grandeur of the Boboli Gardens or enjoying a quiet afternoon in the Rose Garden, these green spaces provide the perfect opportunity to relax and recharge during your time in Florence. They are easily accessible on foot or via public transportation, making them an essential part of any visit to the city.

CHAPTER 5
TUSCAN CITIES BEYOND FLORENCE
Pisa: The Leaning Tower and Beyond

A trip to Tuscany wouldn't be complete without visiting Pisa, home to the famous Leaning Tower. But Pisa has so much more to offer beyond its iconic tower. Whether you're drawn by its fascinating history, stunning architecture, or charming atmosphere, Pisa is worth exploring.

The Leaning Tower is, of course, the most popular attraction in Pisa. Located in Piazza dei Miracoli, this freestanding bell tower has been leaning for centuries due to unstable ground beneath it. The tower, which is part of the Pisa Cathedral, started tilting during its construction in the 12th century, and efforts to stabilize it have kept it standing today. Visitors can climb the 294 steps to the top for spectacular views over the city. The experience of standing on the slanting tower is thrilling and offers a unique perspective of Pisa.

Right next to the tower, you'll find the Pisa Cathedral, also known as the Duomo. With its beautiful white marble façade and intricate architectural details, the cathedral is a masterpiece of Romanesque art. Inside, you'll see stunning mosaics, artworks, and the famous pulpit designed by Giovanni Pisano. The cathedral's peaceful atmosphere is a lovely contrast to the busy square outside.

The Baptistery of St. John is another highlight in the Piazza dei Miracoli. It's the largest baptistery in Italy, and its circular structure with elegant Gothic and Romanesque features makes it a striking sight. If you visit inside, you can experience the unique acoustics of the building, which create an impressive echo. Climbing to the upper gallery provides beautiful views of the cathedral and the square.

Once you've seen the famous monuments in Piazza dei Miracoli, take the time to explore Pisa beyond its well-known landmarks. Head into the historic center, where you can wander along the Arno River and discover the city's quieter, less touristy side. The vibrant squares, charming streets, and local markets give you a taste of everyday life in Pisa. Be sure to stop by Piazza dei Cavalieri, once the political heart of medieval Pisa, now a beautiful square surrounded by historic buildings.

The University of Pisa, one of the oldest in Italy, gives the city a lively and youthful energy. You'll find students gathering in cafés and parks, adding to the relaxed and friendly atmosphere. While exploring the city, don't miss Borgo Stretto, a narrow street filled with shops, cafés, and historical buildings. It's the perfect place to grab a coffee or gelato and enjoy a leisurely walk.

For art lovers, the Museo Nazionale di San Matteo is a hidden gem. Located by the river at Piazza San Matteo, it houses a collection of medieval art, including sculptures, paintings, and ceramics from Pisa and Tuscany. It's a peaceful, off-the-beaten-path museum that provides insight into the region's rich artistic history.

If you have time, consider taking a trip to the nearby beach town of Marina di Pisa. Just a short drive from the city, this coastal area offers a beautiful seaside escape with its pebble beaches, calm waters, and fresh seafood restaurants.

Pisa is much more than just the Leaning Tower. From its grand cathedral to its charming streets and vibrant local life, the city has a lot to offer. While most visitors come for the tower, taking the time to explore beyond the famous landmarks will give you a deeper appreciation of Pisa's rich history and culture. It's easy to reach Pisa by train or car from Florence, making it a perfect day trip or a longer stop during your journey through Tuscany.

Siena: The Palio and Gothic Splendor

Siena is a city that seems to have been frozen in time, with its medieval streets and stunning Gothic architecture making it a must-visit destination in Tuscany. One of its most famous events is the Palio, a historic horse race held twice a year in the city's main square, Piazza del Campo. But even beyond the excitement of the Palio, Siena offers so much for visitors to experience, from its rich history to its architectural beauty.

The Palio di Siena is not just a horse race but a tradition that has been passed down for centuries. It takes place on July 2nd and August 16th each year, when different districts (known as "contrade") of Siena compete against each other in a thrilling race around the Piazza del Campo. The square is transformed into a racetrack, and the whole city is caught up in the excitement. The build-up to the race includes parades, flag-waving, and lots of fanfare, giving visitors a glimpse into the strong local pride and the traditions that define Siena. If you're visiting during these dates, witnessing the Palio is an unforgettable experience, but it's important to plan ahead, as the city gets very crowded during this time.

Even when the Palio is not taking place, Piazza del Campo is one of the most beautiful squares in Italy. Its unique shell shape, with brick paving and a gentle slope, gives it a sense of harmony and elegance. At the center of the square, you'll find the Fonte Gaia, a beautiful marble fountain, while the square itself is surrounded by impressive medieval buildings. One of the most prominent is the Palazzo Pubblico, the town hall, which is home to the Civic Museum. Inside, you can see remarkable frescoes, including the famous "Allegory of Good and Bad Government" by Ambrogio Lorenzetti. Climbing the Torre del Mangia, the tall tower attached to the Palazzo, rewards you with incredible views over Siena and the surrounding countryside.

Siena is also known for its stunning Gothic cathedral, the Duomo di Siena. This striking building, with its black-and-white striped marble façade, is one of the finest examples of Italian Gothic architecture. Inside, the cathedral is filled with masterpieces of art, including sculptures by Michelangelo and Bernini, and a floor decorated with intricate marble inlays. Don't miss the Piccolomini Library inside the Duomo, which features vibrant frescoes by Pinturicchio, depicting the life of Pope Pius II. The cathedral also has a fascinating museum that offers access to the "Facciatone," an unfinished part of the building that provides a panoramic view of the city.

Another must-see in Siena is the Basilica di San Domenico. This large, austere church is dedicated to Saint Catherine of Siena, one of Italy's patron saints, and contains relics and artifacts related to her life. It's a peaceful place to reflect, and the view from the church's terrace is one of the best in Siena.

Beyond its famous landmarks, Siena is a city to be savored slowly. Wandering its narrow, winding streets, you'll come across charming little squares, local shops, and cafés where you can sit and enjoy the atmosphere. Siena is known for its delicious Tuscan cuisine, so be sure to try local specialties like pici (thick, hand-rolled pasta), ribollita (a hearty vegetable soup), and the famous panforte, a dense fruit and nut cake that's a Sienese tradition.

For art lovers, the Pinacoteca Nazionale di Siena houses an impressive collection of medieval and Renaissance paintings, with works by artists like Duccio, Simone Martini, and Sano di Pietro. The museum is less crowded than some of the bigger galleries in Florence, making it a quiet place to appreciate Siena's artistic heritage.

Siena's location in the heart of Tuscany also makes it an excellent base for exploring the surrounding countryside. The rolling hills of the Crete Senesi, the vineyards of Chianti, and the charming hill towns of San Gimignano and Montepulciano are all within easy reach, offering a chance to experience the beauty of the Tuscan landscape.

Whether you're drawn by the drama of the Palio or the Gothic splendor of its buildings, Siena is a city that captivates with its rich history, vibrant culture, and timeless beauty. It's easily accessible from Florence by train or bus, and spending a day or more in Siena is an essential part of any trip to Tuscany.

Lucca: Medieval Walls and Charming Streets

Lucca is a beautiful, quiet gem in Tuscany that charms visitors with its well-preserved medieval walls and picturesque streets. Located just a short distance from Florence and Pisa, it's a city where history and modern life come together in a seamless blend, offering an experience that feels both relaxed and timeless.

One of the most striking features of Lucca is its intact city walls. Built during the Renaissance, these walls are not just a historical monument, but they also serve as a wide, tree-lined promenade that encircles the old town. You can walk or cycle along the walls and enjoy fantastic views of the city and surrounding countryside. It's a peaceful place for a stroll, and you'll find locals walking their dogs, families out for a leisurely bike ride, and visitors pausing to take in the scenery. The fact that Lucca's walls have been turned into a public park is a testament to the city's commitment to preserving its history while making it part of everyday life.

Inside the walls, Lucca's historic center is a maze of narrow, winding streets and charming piazzas. The city's Roman origins are still visible in its layout, and you'll feel like you've stepped back in time as you explore. Piazza dell'Anfiteatro, one of the most famous squares in Lucca, is a perfect example of this. It was once a Roman amphitheater, and its circular shape remains intact, with buildings now surrounding the square where gladiators once fought. Today, it's filled with cafés and restaurants, making it a great spot to relax, sip an espresso, and soak in the atmosphere.

Lucca is also home to a number of beautiful churches, each with its own story. The Duomo di San Martino is the city's cathedral, and its Romanesque façade is both grand and elegant. Inside, you'll find several important artworks, including the famous Volto Santo, a wooden crucifix that, according to legend, was carved by Nicodemus, a contemporary of Jesus. The Basilica of San Frediano is another must-see, with its striking golden mosaic on the façade and its interior filled with beautiful frescoes.

As you wander through the streets of Lucca, you'll notice the city's many towers. In the medieval period, wealthy families would build towers as a sign of their power and influence. Today, the most famous of these is the Torre Guinigi, which is unique because it has trees growing on top. Climbing to the top of this tower gives you a fantastic panoramic view of Lucca, and standing under the oak trees at the top, you'll feel like you're in a little garden above the city.

Lucca also has a strong musical heritage. It's the birthplace of the famous composer Giacomo Puccini, and his music is still celebrated in the city today. You can visit Puccini's childhood home, which has been turned into a museum, and learn more about his life and works. There are also regular concerts held in Lucca's churches and theaters, featuring performances of Puccini's operas as well as other classical music.

One of the joys of visiting Lucca is simply exploring its streets at your own pace. The city isn't as crowded as some of Tuscany's other destinations, so you can take your time, discovering hidden corners, local shops, and little squares without feeling rushed. Lucca is known for its high-quality artisanal goods, from handmade leather products to locally crafted jewelry, so it's a great place to pick up unique souvenirs.

If you're a food lover, Lucca won't disappoint. The city's cuisine is rooted in Tuscan tradition, with an emphasis on simple, high-quality ingredients. You'll find plenty of trattorias serving hearty local dishes like farro soup, tordelli (a type of stuffed pasta), and buccellato, a sweet bread with raisins and aniseed. Pair your meal with a glass of local wine, and you've got the perfect end to a day of exploring.

Lucca's location also makes it an excellent base for further adventures in Tuscany. You can easily take day trips to nearby towns like Pisa, or venture into the stunning hills and vineyards of the surrounding countryside.

In Lucca, history feels alive, but it's not overwhelming. It's a city where you can immerse yourself in the past while enjoying the slower pace of life that the locals treasure. Whether you're cycling along the walls, climbing a medieval tower, or sitting in a quiet square with a gelato in hand, Lucca offers a peaceful and memorable Tuscan experience.

Arezzo: Art, Antiques, and History

Arezzo is a captivating city in Tuscany that often flies under the radar compared to its more famous neighbors like Florence and Siena, but it's a hidden treasure waiting to be explored. Known for its rich history, remarkable art, and vibrant antique scene, Arezzo offers visitors a glimpse into authentic Tuscan life without the large tourist crowds.

As you walk through Arezzo's streets, you can feel the weight of history surrounding you. The city has ancient origins, once a major Etruscan settlement before becoming a thriving Roman town. Today, its medieval character is beautifully preserved, with stone-paved streets, grand piazzas, and old churches that tell the story of centuries past. One of the first places to explore is the Piazza Grande, the heart of the city. This sloping square, framed by medieval buildings, is where life in Arezzo comes alive, especially during the city's famous monthly antique market. If you love discovering unique pieces from the past, this market is a dream come true. You'll find everything from furniture and jewelry to vintage books and artwork, with vendors filling the square and surrounding streets with treasures from bygone eras.

But it's not just antiques that make Arezzo special. The city is also home to some incredible works of art, most notably the frescoes of Piero della Francesca in the Basilica di San Francesco. These frescoes, known as The Legend of the True Cross, are considered masterpieces of the Italian Renaissance, and seeing them up close is a moving experience. The way Piero della Francesca captured light, perspective, and emotion in his scenes is breathtaking, and art lovers from around the world come to Arezzo just to admire this series. The basilica itself is a serene and beautiful space, with its simple stone interior providing the perfect backdrop to these timeless frescoes.

Arezzo's artistic heritage doesn't end with Piero della Francesca. The city has also been the home of many other influential figures, including the poet Petrarch and the architect and artist Giorgio Vasari. Vasari's house, now a museum, offers a fascinating insight into the life and works of this important Renaissance figure. Inside, you can see frescoes and paintings that Vasari created for his own home, along with other personal artifacts. It's a small but intriguing stop for those interested in the art and architecture of the Renaissance.

Another key site in Arezzo is the Cathedral of San Donato, a Gothic gem with an imposing façade and a stunning interior. Inside, you'll find more of Piero della Francesca's work, including the beautiful fresco of Mary Magdalene. The cathedral also boasts incredible stained glass windows that fill the space with colorful light, creating a peaceful and contemplative atmosphere. The bell tower offers fantastic views over the city and the surrounding countryside, making it well worth the climb.

Arezzo is also a city where tradition and history are alive and well. One of the best times to visit is during the Giostra del Saracino, a medieval jousting tournament held in June and September. This lively event brings the whole city together in a colorful celebration of its past, with knights in armor competing in the main square as crowds cheer them on. It's a fantastic way to experience the local culture and feel the deep connection that Arezzo's residents have to their history.

While Arezzo's historic and artistic offerings are impressive, it's also a wonderful place to simply enjoy the Tuscan lifestyle. The city has plenty of lovely cafés, wine bars, and trattorias where you can sit back and savor the local flavors. Tuscan cuisine is all about simplicity and quality, and in Arezzo, you can taste some of the best. Look out for dishes like ribollita, a hearty bread and vegetable soup, and tagliatelle with wild boar sauce, which is a local favorite. And of course, no meal in Tuscany is complete without a glass of local wine, and Arezzo's surrounding vineyards produce some excellent varieties.

Arezzo is also an ideal base for exploring other parts of Tuscany. From here, you can easily reach nearby towns and villages, like Cortona, another historic gem perched on a hillside, or the Val di Chiana region, known for its beautiful landscapes and vineyards.

Arezzo is a city that offers a little bit of everything – history, art, culture, and a relaxed, authentic atmosphere. Whether you're admiring Renaissance frescoes, hunting for antiques, or simply wandering its medieval streets, Arezzo gives you the chance to experience Tuscany at its most charming and genuine.

Livorno: The Port City with a Character

Livorno, a lively port city on the western coast of Tuscany, is often overshadowed by the more famous cities in the region. However, Livorno has its own unique character and charm, making it worth a visit, especially for those interested in experiencing an authentic coastal atmosphere. This city has a rich maritime history, and its location along the Tyrrhenian Sea gives it a fresh, breezy vibe quite different from the more inland Tuscan towns.

As soon as you arrive in Livorno, you'll notice its connection to the sea. The city's port is one of the largest in Italy, bustling with ships, ferries, and yachts. This maritime influence shapes much of Livorno's character, from its seafood cuisine to the laid-back lifestyle of its residents. Walking along the harbor, you'll see fishermen bringing in their daily catch, with the salty air and the sound of seagulls creating the perfect seaside backdrop.

Livorno's history as a port city is deeply intertwined with its role as a cosmopolitan hub. During the Renaissance, it became a melting pot of cultures, as merchants from all over the Mediterranean settled here. This has left a fascinating mark on the city's architecture and culture. The Venetian-style canals that cut through parts of Livorno are a reminder of this vibrant past. Known as the Quartiere Venezia, this neighborhood is one of the most picturesque parts of the city. You can explore its narrow streets and canals by foot or even by boat, which is a great way to see Livorno from a different perspective.

One of the highlights of any visit to Livorno is its famous Mercato Centrale. This bustling market is housed in an impressive 19th-century building and is the perfect place to sample the city's freshest produce. Inside, you'll find everything from local cheeses and cured meats to an incredible selection of seafood. Don't miss the opportunity to try cacciucco, Livorno's signature dish. It's a hearty fish stew made with a variety of seafood, tomatoes, garlic, and red wine, served with toasted bread. It's the ultimate comfort food and gives you a real taste of the city's culinary traditions.

Another must-see in Livorno is the Terrazza Mascagni, a large, checkerboard-patterned promenade along the waterfront. It's a popular spot for both locals and visitors, offering stunning views of the sea and a perfect place for a leisurely stroll. During the warmer months, you'll often see families and couples enjoying the sunset here, with the sea breeze adding to the relaxing atmosphere. The Terrazza is also close to several beach clubs where you can rent a sunbed and spend the day by the sea.

Livorno's fortresses are also worth exploring. The Fortezza Vecchia and Fortezza Nuova are two historic forts that once protected the city from invaders. The Fortezza Vecchia, located near the harbor, is a symbol of Livorno's strength as a port city and offers great views of the port and the city skyline. The Fortezza Nuova, surrounded by the Venetian canals, is a peaceful park today, perfect for a relaxing break amidst its old walls.

For art lovers, the Museo Civico Giovanni Fattori is a must. Located in Villa Mimbelli, this museum is dedicated to the works of the famous Macchiaioli painters, a group of 19th-century Italian artists who predated the Impressionists. The villa itself is a beautiful example of 19th-century architecture, with lush gardens where you can take a peaceful walk after exploring the art inside.

Livorno is also known for its sense of fun and quirkiness, best seen during the Effetto Venezia festival, which takes place every summer in the Quartiere Venezia. The entire neighborhood is transformed into a lively celebration of music, theater, art, and food, with performances taking place along the canals and in the streets. It's a fantastic time to experience the city's creative and vibrant side.

Beyond the city, Livorno is a gateway to some of Tuscany's most beautiful coastal destinations. From here, you can easily take a ferry to the nearby islands of the Tuscan Archipelago, such as Elba, famous for its crystal-clear waters and stunning beaches. It's also a short drive to the beautiful beach towns of Castiglioncello and Quercianella, where you can relax by the sea or enjoy some excellent seafood in the local restaurants.

Livorno is a city with a distinctive personality, shaped by its maritime history and multicultural past. Its mix of history, culture, and coastal beauty makes it a great destination for travelers looking to explore a different side of Tuscany. Whether you're enjoying the local seafood, wandering through its Venetian-style canals, or taking in the sea views from the Terrazza Mascagni, Livorno offers a refreshing and authentic Tuscan experience by the sea.

Pistoia: Off-the-Beaten-Path Discovery

Pistoia is a hidden gem in Tuscany, often overlooked by travelers in favor of more famous cities like Florence and Siena. However, if you're seeking a quieter, more authentic Tuscan experience, Pistoia is a wonderful place to explore. Its medieval charm, fascinating history, and lack of heavy tourist crowds make it the perfect off-the-beaten-path discovery.

As you wander through Pistoia's narrow streets, the first thing you'll notice is its well-preserved medieval architecture. The town's heart is the Piazza del Duomo, an impressive square surrounded by historic buildings that immediately transport you back in time. The Cathedral of San Zeno, with its stunning Romanesque facade, is the centerpiece. Inside, you'll find beautiful frescoes and a peaceful atmosphere. Next to the cathedral is the Battistero di San Giovanni, a striking octagonal baptistery made of white and green marble. Climbing to the top offers lovely views of the town and surrounding hills.

Pistoia is also home to one of the oldest and most fascinating underground spaces in Tuscany. The Pistoia Sotterranea is a network of tunnels beneath the city, originally used for water drainage and later for other purposes. A guided tour will take you through these ancient pathways, where you'll learn about the town's history and see remnants of its medieval past.

A visit to Pistoia wouldn't be complete without a stop at the Ospedale del Ceppo, an ancient hospital dating back to the 13th century. The building's most notable feature is the beautiful glazed terracotta frieze on its facade, created by the

Della Robbia family, famous for their ceramic works. The frieze illustrates scenes of healing and care, reflecting the hospital's original purpose. Today, part of the hospital has been turned into a museum where you can explore its history and the incredible art inside.

For art lovers, the Marino Marini Museum is a must. Marino Marini was a renowned 20th-century sculptor born in Pistoia, and this museum houses a large collection of his works, including his famous sculptures of horses and riders. The museum is located in a restored medieval building, and the combination of contemporary art with ancient architecture creates a unique atmosphere.

Pistoia also has a strong connection to nature. Just outside the town, you'll find the Pistoia Zoo, which is great for a family visit. Set in a large green park, the zoo is home to a variety of animals from all over the world, offering a peaceful escape from the hustle and bustle of the city.

If you visit Pistoia on a Wednesday or Saturday, you'll have the chance to experience the local market in Piazza della Sala. This vibrant market is one of the oldest in Tuscany and is still a hub of daily life for locals. Stalls are filled with fresh fruits, vegetables, cheeses, and meats, making it the perfect place to pick up some local produce or simply enjoy the lively atmosphere. Surrounding the square, you'll find cozy cafes and restaurants where you can relax with a coffee or try some traditional Tuscan dishes.

Food in Pistoia is simple, hearty, and rooted in tradition. The town is known for its local specialties such as necci, savory chestnut pancakes often filled with ricotta cheese, and carcerato, a rustic soup made with beans and vegetables. You'll find plenty of trattorias in town where you can enjoy these dishes in an authentic setting, often prepared using recipes that have been passed down for generations.

While Pistoia may not have the grand galleries and museums of Florence, its charm lies in its authenticity. The town's relaxed pace allows you to enjoy Tuscany without the crowds, offering a more personal connection to the region's history and culture. Exploring its historic streets, visiting its unique museums, and savoring its local cuisine all make for a deeply rewarding experience.

Pistoia is also well connected to other parts of Tuscany. It's just a short train ride from Florence, making it easy to include in your itinerary. Whether you visit for a day or choose to stay longer, Pistoia offers a glimpse of Tuscany that's refreshingly off the typical tourist trail. With its rich history, quiet beauty, and welcoming atmosphere, it's a destination worth discovering.

CHAPTER 6.
THE TUSCAN COUNTRYSIDE
Chianti: Rolling Hills, Vineyards, and Wineries

Chianti is the picture-perfect image of Tuscany that often comes to mind – rolling hills covered in vineyards, charming villages, and an abundance of wineries producing some of the best wine in the world. Located between Florence and Siena, the Chianti region is a haven for wine lovers and those seeking the quintessential Tuscan countryside experience.

As you travel through Chianti, you'll immediately notice the landscape's breathtaking beauty. The gently rolling hills are covered with rows of grapevines, olive groves, and cypress trees, with stone farmhouses and medieval villages dotting the horizon. This is the land where Chianti Classico, the region's famous red wine, is produced, and nearly every hillside is home to a vineyard or winery.

Visiting Chianti isn't just about tasting wine, though that's certainly one of the highlights. The region is perfect for exploring at a leisurely pace, whether by car, bike, or even on foot. Winding roads lead through picturesque scenery, and each turn reveals another stunning view or a charming village waiting to be discovered. Towns like Greve in Chianti, Radda in Chianti, and Castellina in Chianti are some of the main stops along the way, each with its own unique charm and history.

Greve in Chianti is often considered the gateway to the region. Its triangular piazza, Piazza Matteotti, is the heart of the town, lined with cafes, wine shops, and local artisan stores. It's a great place to start your journey and sample some of the local specialties, like fresh pecorino cheese, cured meats, and, of course, wine. The town is home to several wine cellars where you can taste Chianti Classico and learn more about its production.

Radda in Chianti is another must-visit town, perched on a hill with stunning views over the vineyards below. Its medieval walls and narrow streets give it a historic feel, and it's a perfect place to take a relaxing stroll. Radda is also known for its wine cellars, and many wineries nearby offer tastings and tours.

Castellina in Chianti is rich in history, with its roots going back to the Etruscans. The town's Rocca, or fortress, dominates the skyline and offers incredible views of the surrounding countryside. Beneath the town, you'll find an ancient tunnel, the Via delle Volte, where you can walk and feel the history beneath your feet. Like the other towns in Chianti, Castellina is surrounded by vineyards, and many of the local wineries offer tours and tastings.

One of the best ways to experience Chianti is to visit the wineries themselves. Many of them are family-owned estates that have been producing wine for generations. These wineries often offer guided tours where you can learn about the winemaking process, from the vineyards where the grapes are grown to the cellars where the wine is aged. At the end of the tour, you'll have the chance to taste their wines, often paired with local products like olive oil, cheese, and cured meats.

Some of the most famous wineries in Chianti include Castello di Ama, known for its contemporary art installations as well as its wine, and Castello di Brolio, one of the oldest wineries in the region. Visiting these estates allows you to immerse yourself in the history and culture of Chianti, while also enjoying some of the finest wines in the world.

If you're interested in learning more about the local wine, consider visiting the Chianti Classico Wine Consortium in Greve. Here, you can learn all about the Chianti Classico label and what makes these wines unique. The black rooster, or "Gallo Nero," is the symbol of Chianti Classico and guarantees that the wine comes from the designated production area and meets the strict quality standards set by the consortium.

While wine is undoubtedly the main attraction in Chianti, the region is also known for its excellent cuisine. Traditional Tuscan dishes like bistecca alla Fiorentina (Florentine steak), ribollita (a hearty vegetable soup), and wild boar are commonly served in local trattorias and restaurants. Many of these eateries are located in beautiful settings, often with outdoor terraces overlooking the vineyards. Dining in Chianti is a wonderful way to enjoy the local flavors while soaking in the region's natural beauty.

For those who love the outdoors, Chianti offers plenty of opportunities for hiking, cycling, and even horseback riding. Several trails wind through the vineyards and forests, offering spectacular views of the countryside. Cycling is particularly popular here, and you'll often see cyclists enjoying the scenic roads that link the towns and villages. Whether you prefer a gentle walk or a more challenging hike, the landscapes of Chianti are sure to impress.

The best time to visit Chianti is in the late spring or early autumn when the weather is pleasant, and the vineyards are at their most beautiful. Autumn is especially wonderful because it's harvest season, and many wineries host special events and festivals celebrating the grape harvest. It's a festive time to visit and a chance to see the winemaking process in full swing.

Chianti is a region that invites you to slow down, savor the flavors of Tuscany, and enjoy the simple pleasures of life. Whether you're sipping wine in a vineyard, exploring a medieval village, or enjoying a meal with a view, Chianti offers an unforgettable experience that embodies the best of Tuscany.

Val d'Orcia: Scenic Drives and Picture-Perfect Landscapes

Val d'Orcia is one of the most breathtaking regions in Tuscany, known for its rolling hills, cypress-lined roads, and vast wheat fields that seem to stretch endlessly into the horizon. This area, a UNESCO World Heritage Site, feels like stepping into a postcard with its picture-perfect landscapes and charming hilltop towns. It's a place where you'll find peace, beauty, and a deep sense of connection to the land.

The best way to experience Val d'Orcia is by car, allowing you the freedom to explore the scenic routes at your own pace. As you drive through the countryside, you'll notice how the landscape changes with the seasons. In the spring, the hills are lush and green, dotted with wildflowers, while in the summer, golden fields of wheat and sunflowers cover the land. The famous rows of cypress trees guide your way along the winding roads, making each turn a perfect photo opportunity.

One of the most iconic drives in Val d'Orcia is the road from San Quirico d'Orcia to Pienza. This route is straight out of a movie, with its gently rolling hills, isolated farmhouses, and stunning panoramas. As you make your way along this road, you'll see why so many artists and photographers are drawn to this region. It's also one of the most photographed areas in Tuscany, especially in the early morning or late afternoon when the soft light casts long shadows over the landscape.

San Quirico d'Orcia is a wonderful town to start your journey. Its medieval walls, narrow streets, and historic architecture give it a timeless feel. The town's main attraction is the beautiful Horti Leonini gardens, a perfect place for a peaceful stroll before heading out into the countryside.

From San Quirico, it's a short drive to Pienza, a jewel of the Renaissance. Pienza was designed by Pope Pius II to be the "ideal city" and is known for its stunning architecture, including the Palazzo Piccolomini and the Duomo. But beyond the buildings, it's the views from the town's walls that will leave you breathless. Looking out over the Val d'Orcia from Pienza is like gazing into a painting. The vast, open landscape below seems almost untouched, with the occasional farmhouse or vineyard breaking up the rolling hills.

If you're looking for another scenic drive, head towards Montalcino, famous for its Brunello wine. The drive to Montalcino takes you through more of Val d'Orcia's beautiful countryside, and once you arrive, you can explore the town's fortress and enjoy a glass of world-class wine. The views from Montalcino are just as stunning, with vineyards and olive groves stretching out as far as the eye can see.

One of the highlights of visiting Val d'Orcia is the thermal baths in Bagno Vignoni. This tiny village is unique because its central square is actually a large thermal pool. The ancient Romans used these hot springs, and today, visitors can still enjoy the warm, healing waters. Nearby, there are also several modern spas where you can relax and unwind in the natural thermal pools while surrounded by the tranquil countryside.

Val d'Orcia is also famous for its food. The region is known for its pecorino cheese, which is produced in many of the small farms around Pienza. You'll find this delicious cheese in local markets and restaurants, often served with honey or fresh pears. It's a must-try when visiting the area, along with other Tuscan specialties like pici pasta, wild boar, and locally grown truffles.

For those who enjoy hiking or cycling, Val d'Orcia offers plenty of opportunities to explore the countryside on foot or by bike. Several trails wind through the hills and along the cypress-lined roads, offering incredible views of the landscape. The Eroica, a famous cycling event, takes place in this region, and the route is open to cyclists throughout the year. Whether you're an experienced hiker or just looking for a leisurely walk, the peaceful surroundings and fresh air make it a perfect way to spend a day.

Val d'Orcia is a place to slow down, breathe in the beauty of the land, and enjoy the simple pleasures of life. Whether you're driving through the scenic roads, tasting the local wines, or taking in the views from a hilltop town, you'll feel a deep connection to the history and culture of Tuscany. This region has a way of capturing your heart, and it's easy to see why so many visitors fall in love with the enchanting landscapes of Val d'Orcia.

Maremma: Tuscany's Wild Coastline

Maremma is Tuscany's untamed coastline, a region where rugged landscapes meet the Mediterranean Sea, offering a striking contrast to the rolling hills and vineyards that many associate with the area. It's a place where you can experience Tuscany's wild side, with long stretches of unspoiled beaches, dense forests, and charming villages that have preserved their ancient traditions. Maremma is ideal for travelers seeking a more off-the-beaten-path destination, full of natural beauty and authentic experiences.

The coastline here is simply stunning. One of the highlights is the Parco della Maremma, a protected natural reserve that stretches along the coast. This park is home to a variety of wildlife, including wild boar, deer, and even the iconic Maremman cattle. The landscape is diverse, with sandy beaches, rocky cliffs, and vast pine forests. For nature lovers, the park offers numerous trails that you can explore on foot, by bike, or even on horseback. The best time to visit is during spring or early autumn when the weather is mild, and you can fully appreciate the serenity of the park.

The beaches of Maremma are some of the most beautiful in Tuscany. One of the most popular is Cala Violina, a secluded cove with crystal-clear waters and fine, white sand that, legend says, makes a violin-like sound when you walk on it. Getting to Cala Violina requires a short hike through the forest, but the effort is well worth it. The beach is perfect for a relaxing day by the sea, with calm waters that are great for swimming and snorkeling. Another great option is Marina di Alberese, located within the Parco della Maremma. This beach feels wild and untouched, with a long stretch of sand backed by dunes and pine trees. It's less crowded than some of the more touristy beaches, making it a peaceful escape.

Maremma's towns and villages are equally captivating. One of the most picturesque is Pitigliano, a town perched dramatically on a tufa rock, with its medieval houses seeming to cling to the cliffside. Pitigliano has a rich history, including a significant Jewish heritage, which you can explore in its Synagogue and Jewish Museum. Walking through the narrow streets of this town feels like stepping back in time, and the views from the town's walls over the surrounding countryside are breathtaking.

Nearby, the towns of Sovana and Sorano are also worth visiting. Sovana is known for its Etruscan tombs, while Sorano's ancient houses blend seamlessly with the rocky landscape. These towns are quieter than the more famous destinations in Tuscany, but their charm lies in their authenticity and the sense of history that pervades every corner.

If you're interested in history and archaeology, the archaeological site of Roselle offers a fascinating glimpse into the past. This ancient Etruscan city is remarkably well-preserved, with ruins of houses, walls, and an amphitheater that you can explore at your leisure. It's a quiet, peaceful site, where you can wander among the remnants of a civilization that once thrived in this region.

For those looking to unwind, the thermal baths of Saturnia are a must-visit. These natural hot springs are famous for their warm, sulfur-rich waters, which have been used for their healing properties since ancient times. The thermal pools cascade down a series of limestone terraces, creating a stunning setting to relax and rejuvenate. Best of all, the natural pools are free to visit, though there is also a nearby luxury spa if you're looking for a more pampered experience.

Maremma is also a paradise for food lovers. The region's cuisine is hearty and rustic, reflecting the agricultural roots of the area. Dishes often feature wild game, such as wild boar, which is used in everything from stews to pasta sauces. The local cheese, Pecorino di Maremma, is another highlight, as are the wines produced in the region, such as the Morellino di Scansano. Many restaurants in the area focus on using local, seasonal ingredients, so you're sure to enjoy fresh and flavorful meals.

One of the best ways to explore Maremma is by car, as it gives you the freedom to discover the region's hidden gems at your own pace. The roads wind through vineyards, olive groves, and forests, offering scenic views at every turn. Whether you're stopping to visit a small village, hiking in the hills, or enjoying a meal at a family-run trattoria, you'll get a true sense of Maremma's authenticity and natural beauty.

In Maremma, Tuscany reveals a wilder, more rugged side, far from the well-trodden paths of Florence and Chianti. It's a place where nature reigns supreme, where the pace of life is slower, and where every corner holds a new discovery. Whether you're drawn by the allure of its beaches, the history of its towns, or the tranquility of its countryside, Maremma offers an unforgettable experience.

Casentino: Forests, Castles, and Sacred Sites

Casentino, a captivating valley in Tuscany, invites you to explore its rich landscapes, historical castles, and sacred sites. Nestled between the rolling hills and dense forests, this region offers a serene retreat into nature and history, perfect for travelers seeking a blend of outdoor adventure and cultural immersion.

One of the standout features of Casentino is its lush, ancient forests. The Casentino Forests, Monte Falterona, and Campigna National Park cover a vast area of over 36,000 hectares and provide a stunning backdrop for outdoor activities. This park is a haven for hikers and nature enthusiasts. Trails wind through dense woodlands, past bubbling streams, and up to panoramic viewpoints that offer sweeping vistas of the Tuscan countryside. The park is home to a diverse range of wildlife, including deer, wild boar, and various bird species. Whether you're looking for a peaceful walk or a more challenging hike, the forest offers something for everyone.

Among the highlights of the Casentino Forests is the picturesque area around the Acquacheta Waterfall. The waterfall cascades down a rocky cliff, creating a serene and refreshing spot for visitors. The hike to the waterfall is relatively easy and offers beautiful views of the surrounding forest. Another scenic spot is the Vallombrosa Abbey, set amidst the forest. This historic abbey, founded in the 11th century, is known for its peaceful atmosphere and beautiful gardens.

Casentino is also renowned for its castles and fortresses, each telling its own tale of the region's past. One of the most notable is the Castle of Poppi. This medieval fortress stands atop a hill overlooking the town of Poppi and offers breathtaking views of the surrounding valley. The castle's interiors are equally impressive, with well-preserved rooms and artifacts that provide a glimpse into medieval life. The castle's library is particularly noteworthy, housing a collection of ancient manuscripts.

Another fascinating castle is the Castle of Romena, located near the village of the same name. This castle, though partly in ruins, still exudes a strong sense of history. The walls and towers provide a dramatic setting for exploring and imagining the castle's past. From the castle's vantage points, you can enjoy panoramic views of the Casentino landscape.

In addition to its natural and historical attractions, Casentino is home to several sacred sites that offer spiritual and historical significance. One of the most important is the Sanctuary of La Verna. This holy site is deeply associated with Saint Francis of Assisi, who retreated here to meditate and pray. The sanctuary is set in a peaceful, forested area and includes a chapel and a hermitage. Visitors can explore the sanctuary's tranquil grounds, visit the chapel, and reflect on the significance of this sacred space.

The Hermitage of Camaldoli is another notable religious site in the region. Founded in the 11th century by Saint Romuald, this hermitage is known for its spiritual significance and stunning location amidst the forest. The complex includes a monastery, a church, and various walking paths that lead through the surrounding woods. The peaceful environment and the opportunity to witness monastic life make Camaldoli a unique and meaningful destination.

For a taste of local culture and tradition, the town of Arezzo, just a short drive from Casentino, offers charming streets, lively markets, and historical landmarks. Arezzo is known for its antique shops and art galleries, making it a great place to explore Tuscany's artistic heritage.

As you travel through Casentino, you'll find that renting a car is the most convenient way to get around. The roads are well-maintained, and having a car allows you to easily reach the various attractions spread throughout the region. Be sure to take your time driving through the picturesque countryside, where you'll come across hidden villages and scenic viewpoints that are well worth stopping for.

Casentino offers a rich tapestry of experiences, from its enchanting forests and majestic castles to its sacred sites and charming towns. It's a region where nature, history, and spirituality intertwine, providing a peaceful and immersive travel experience. Whether you're hiking through ancient woodlands, exploring medieval fortresses, or visiting serene religious sites, Casentino reveals the diverse and captivating beauty of Tuscany.

The Hilltop Towns of Tuscany: San Gimignano, Volterra, and Montepulciano

Exploring the hilltop towns of Tuscany offers a journey back in time through charming medieval streets, stunning vistas, and rich local traditions. Among these towns, San Gimignano, Volterra, and Montepulciano stand out as captivating destinations, each with its own unique allure.

San Gimignano, often referred to as the "Medieval Manhattan," is famous for its skyline of medieval towers. As you wander through its narrow streets, you'll be greeted by the towering structures that have earned it this nickname. The town's most iconic feature is its well-preserved medieval architecture, with numerous towers that were once built by wealthy families to showcase their power and prestige. A stroll through the town will lead you to the Piazza della Cisterna, a beautiful square surrounded by historic buildings. The town is also renowned for its white wine, Vernaccia di San Gimignano, which you can taste at local wine bars or restaurants. The Collegiata, a Romanesque church, features stunning frescoes that provide a glimpse into the town's artistic heritage.

Volterra, with its Etruscan roots, offers a different flavor of Tuscan history. This ancient town is perched on a hill and is surrounded by well-preserved medieval walls. As you enter Volterra, you'll be struck by its historical ambiance. The Roman Theatre, dating back to the 1st century BC, provides a fascinating glimpse into ancient Roman life. The town is also known for its alabaster production, and you can visit workshops where artisans craft intricate pieces from this local stone. The Piazza dei Priori, Volterra's main square, is a lively place surrounded by historic buildings, including the Palazzo dei Priori and the Palazzo Pretorio. Walking through the town's narrow streets, you'll discover hidden squares and charming shops selling local crafts.

Montepulciano, famous for its wine and Renaissance architecture, is another hilltop gem worth visiting. Known as the "Pearl of the 16th Century," Montepulciano boasts elegant palaces, churches, and squares. The town is renowned for its Vino Nobile di Montepulciano, a rich red wine that has been produced here for centuries. You can visit local wineries to sample this acclaimed wine and learn about its production. The Piazza Grande, the town's main square, is surrounded by impressive buildings, including the Palazzo Comunale and the Cathedral of Montepulciano. The town's medieval streets are perfect for exploring on foot, with plenty of shops, cafes, and restaurants to enjoy. Don't miss a visit to the Cantina de' Ricci, a historic wine cellar located in a beautiful underground setting.

Getting to these hilltop towns is relatively straightforward if you have a car. The roads are well-maintained, and driving through the Tuscan countryside provides beautiful views of rolling hills and vineyards. If you prefer public transport, you can reach these towns by bus or train from larger cities like Florence or Siena. Each town is well-signposted, and once you arrive, parking is usually available on the outskirts, with easy access to the town centers.

San Gimignano, Volterra, and Montepulciano each offer a unique glimpse into Tuscany's rich history and culture. San Gimignano enchants with its medieval towers and local wine, Volterra showcases its ancient Etruscan and Roman heritage alongside alabaster crafts, and Montepulciano invites you to savor fine wines while exploring Renaissance architecture. Visiting these hilltop towns allows you to experience the diverse charm of Tuscany and enjoy its scenic beauty, historical depth, and local traditions.

CHAPTER U7.
TUSCANY' WINE REGION

Introduction to Tuscan Wines

Tuscan wines are renowned for their quality and diversity, embodying the rich heritage and unique flavors of Italy's most celebrated wine region. The region's landscape, with its rolling hills, sun-drenched vineyards, and varied soils, creates the perfect conditions for producing exceptional wines. When you dive into Tuscan wines, you're not just savoring a drink; you're experiencing centuries of tradition, craftsmanship, and the very essence of Tuscany.

At the heart of Tuscan winemaking is Sangiovese, a grape variety that thrives in the region and forms the backbone of many of its most famous wines. The Sangiovese grape is known for its vibrant acidity, rich fruit flavors, and ability to age gracefully. It is the primary component in renowned wines like Chianti, Brunello di Montalcino, and Vino Nobile di Montepulciano. Each of these wines showcases the grape's versatility and the distinctive characteristics of the various sub-regions within Tuscany.

Chianti is perhaps the most famous Tuscan wine, known for its bright cherry flavors and slightly spicy notes. It originates from the Chianti region, which is situated between Florence and Siena. Chianti wines range from light and easy-drinking to complex and robust, with several classifications such as Chianti Classico and Chianti Riserva indicating the wine's quality and aging potential. The Chianti Classico zone, with its signature black rooster logo, is known for producing some of the finest examples of this wine.

Brunello di Montalcino is another standout Tuscan wine, made exclusively from Sangiovese grapes grown around the hilltop town of Montalcino. This wine is celebrated for its deep, rich flavors of dark fruit, tobacco, and earthy notes. Brunello is known for its aging potential, often requiring several years in the bottle before it reaches its peak. It is a wine that embodies the elegance and complexity of Tuscan winemaking.

Vino Nobile di Montepulciano hails from the town of Montepulciano and is made primarily from Sangiovese, though it can include small amounts of other local grape varieties. This wine is known for its deep color, rich texture, and flavors of ripe fruit and spices. Vino Nobile offers a balance of power and finesse, making it a favorite among wine enthusiasts.

In addition to these renowned reds, Tuscany also produces excellent white wines. Vernaccia di San Gimignano is a notable white wine from the San Gimignano region, known for its crisp acidity and floral, citrusy flavors. It is a refreshing wine that pairs well with a variety of dishes, especially seafood and light pasta.

Exploring Tuscan wines involves more than just tasting the wines themselves. It's also about experiencing the picturesque vineyards where these wines are produced. Many wineries in Tuscany welcome visitors for tours and tastings, providing insights into the winemaking process and the chance to enjoy stunning views of the countryside. When visiting, you can learn about the traditional methods of winemaking, see the aging cellars, and meet the passionate individuals who craft these exceptional wines.

Tuscan wines offer a rich tapestry of flavors and styles, deeply rooted in the region's history and culture. From the bright and vibrant Chianti to the deep and complex Brunello di Montalcino, each wine reflects the unique characteristics of its terroir. Whether you're savoring a glass of Vino Nobile di Montepulciano or enjoying a crisp Vernaccia, you're indulging in a tradition that has been cherished for centuries. Exploring Tuscan wines is a journey through the heart of Italy, offering a taste of the region's heritage and the beauty of its landscapes.

Chianti Classico: The Heart of Tuscan Wine

Chianti Classico is often considered the heart of Tuscan wine, offering a quintessential taste of the region's winemaking heritage. Nestled between Florence and Siena, this historic wine region has been producing exceptional wines for centuries. When you sip a glass of Chianti Classico, you're experiencing not just a wine, but a piece of Tuscany's rich cultural and agricultural history.

Chianti Classico is made predominantly from Sangiovese grapes, which are known for their bright acidity, cherry flavors, and earthy undertones. This grape variety thrives in the unique climate and soil conditions of the Chianti Classico region, producing wines that are both vibrant and complex.

The Chianti Classico region is distinguished by its black rooster logo, which is a mark of authenticity and quality. This logo can be found on the labels of wines that meet the strict regulations set by the Chianti Classico Consortium. These regulations ensure that the wine is produced from grapes grown in the heart of the Chianti region and follows traditional winemaking practices.

Chianti Classico wines are known for their bright ruby red color and their balanced flavors of red fruit, such as cherry and raspberry, combined with subtle notes of spice and herbs. The wines often have a refreshing acidity and smooth tannins, making them versatile and food-friendly. They pair wonderfully with a variety of dishes, from classic Tuscan pasta and pizza to grilled meats and aged cheeses.

One of the hallmarks of Chianti Classico is its ability to age well. Many Chianti Classico wines benefit from a few years of aging, which allows the flavors to develop further and the tannins to soften. Aged Chianti Classico wines can offer deeper, more complex flavors and a richer, more nuanced character.

When visiting the Chianti Classico region, you'll find many charming wineries and vineyards that welcome visitors for tours and tastings. These visits offer a fantastic opportunity to learn more about the winemaking process, explore the beautiful countryside, and sample some of the best Chianti Classico wines. The scenic landscapes, with their rolling hills and picturesque vineyards, provide a stunning backdrop for your wine experience.

To fully appreciate Chianti Classico, it's worth exploring the local wineries and experiencing the wine firsthand. Many wineries offer guided tours where you can see the vineyards, learn about the winemaking techniques, and enjoy a tasting session. This immersive experience gives you a deeper understanding of what makes Chianti Classico so special and allows you to savor the wine in the place where it is crafted.

Chianti Classico represents the essence of Tuscan winemaking. With its rich history, distinctive flavors, and high-quality production standards, it embodies the spirit of the Chianti region. Whether you're a wine connoisseur or simply looking to enjoy a taste of Tuscany, Chianti Classico offers a memorable and authentic wine experience.

Montalcino: Home of Brunello

Montalcino is renowned as the home of Brunello, one of Italy's most prestigious and celebrated wines. Situated in the heart of Tuscany, this charming hilltop town offers a rich blend of history, culture, and exceptional wine that draws visitors from around the world.

Brunello di Montalcino is a red wine made exclusively from Sangiovese grapes, specifically a local clone known as Brunello. This variety is prized for its deep flavors, robust character, and remarkable aging potential. The wine is known for its dark ruby color, complex aromas of dark fruit, tobacco, and earthy notes, and its full-bodied taste with firm tannins and balanced acidity. Brunello often benefits from years of aging, which enhances its flavors and smooths out its texture, making it a wine to be savored over time.

Montalcino's landscape is characterized by rolling hills and lush vineyards, which create an ideal environment for growing Sangiovese grapes. The town itself is picturesque, with narrow medieval streets, stone buildings, and stunning views of the surrounding countryside. It offers a delightful setting to explore the local culture and, of course, taste some of the finest wines in the region.

Visitors to Montalcino can enjoy guided tours of local wineries and vineyards, where they can see firsthand how Brunello is made. These tours often include visits to the cellars where the wine is aged in oak barrels, and tastings of various Brunello vintages. The experience is educational and immersive, offering insight into the winemaking process and the unique qualities that make Brunello so special.

In addition to wine tasting, Montalcino boasts several charming restaurants and wine bars where you can enjoy local cuisine paired with Brunello. Traditional Tuscan dishes such as pasta with wild boar ragu, roasted meats, and hearty stews are excellent companions to a glass of this exceptional wine. The local eateries often serve dishes made with fresh, local ingredients, enhancing the overall experience of dining in this beautiful region.

The town of Montalcino also hosts various wine festivals and events throughout the year, including the famous "Benvenuto Brunello" festival, which celebrates the new vintage of Brunello. These events offer an opportunity to sample the latest releases, meet local winemakers, and immerse yourself in the vibrant wine culture of the region.

For those interested in exploring further, the surrounding area of Montalcino offers scenic drives and hiking trails with breathtaking views of the vineyards and hills. The landscape is dotted with historic churches, ancient abbeys, and quaint villages that add to the charm of the region.

Montalcino is a must-visit destination for wine enthusiasts and travelers seeking an authentic Tuscan experience. With its renowned Brunello wines, beautiful landscapes, and rich cultural heritage, Montalcino provides a memorable and enriching visit. Whether you're exploring the vineyards, savoring local cuisine, or simply enjoying the picturesque setting, Montalcino offers a true taste of Tuscany's winemaking legacy.

Montepulciano: Vino Nobile

Montepulciano is another gem of Tuscany, known for producing Vino Nobile, a distinguished and highly esteemed red wine. This charming hilltop town, nestled in the rolling hills of southern Tuscany, is celebrated for its rich history, stunning architecture, and, of course, its superb wine.

Vino Nobile di Montepulciano is made primarily from Sangiovese grapes, though it often includes small amounts of other varietals like Canaiolo and Colorino. This wine is recognized for its deep ruby color, complex bouquet of red and black fruits, and subtle hints of spices, tobacco, and earth. The flavor profile is robust yet smooth, with well-integrated tannins and balanced acidity, making it a versatile wine that pairs beautifully with a variety of foods.

The town of Montepulciano itself is a picturesque and well-preserved example of medieval architecture. As you stroll through its narrow, cobblestone streets, you'll encounter Renaissance buildings, ancient churches, and charming squares that offer glimpses into its rich past. The town's skyline is dominated by the impressive Palazzo Comunale, a grand structure that resembles a miniaturized version of Florence's Palazzo Vecchio.

Visiting Montepulciano provides an excellent opportunity to explore local vineyards and wineries where Vino Nobile is crafted. Many of these estates offer guided tours that take you through the winemaking process, from grape harvesting to aging in oak barrels. During these tours, you'll learn about the techniques that contribute to the wine's quality and taste, and you'll have the chance to sample different vintages of Vino

Nobile, experiencing the nuances and variations that come with each year's harvest.

In addition to wine tours, Montepulciano is home to several wine bars and restaurants where you can enjoy Vino Nobile alongside delicious Tuscan cuisine. Local dishes such as pici cacio e pepe (thick pasta with cheese and pepper), Florentine steak, and various hearty stews are perfect complements to this rich and flavorful wine. Dining in Montepulciano often means enjoying meals prepared with fresh, local ingredients, enhancing the overall experience of the region's culinary delights.

Montepulciano also hosts various festivals and events celebrating Vino Nobile and local traditions. One notable event is the "Cantiere Internazionale d'Arte," an international arts festival held each summer, which includes music, theater, and dance performances, creating a vibrant cultural atmosphere. Additionally, the "Bravio delle Botti" is a unique local festival where teams from different neighborhoods race barrels of wine through the streets, adding a fun and competitive spirit to the town's festivities.

For those who love scenic drives and outdoor activities, the surrounding countryside of Montepulciano offers beautiful landscapes of vineyards and rolling hills. Exploring the area by car or bike provides stunning views and opportunities to discover smaller, less-visited towns and vineyards.

Montepulciano is a fantastic destination for anyone interested in experiencing Tuscan wine culture. With its acclaimed Vino Nobile, charming medieval streets, and rich cultural events, Montepulciano offers a delightful and immersive visit.

Whether you're tasting the wine, savoring local dishes, or simply enjoying the picturesque setting, Montepulciano provides a genuine taste of Tuscany's winemaking heritage.

Bolgheri: The Super Tuscans

Bolgheri is a renowned wine region in Tuscany, celebrated for its "Super Tuscan" wines. Located on the Etruscan Coast, this picturesque village and its surrounding vineyards offer a unique glimpse into one of Tuscany's most innovative wine-producing areas. The Super Tuscans are a category of wines that broke traditional rules to create exceptional blends with international appeal.

The Super Tuscans are particularly famous for their use of non-traditional grape varieties. While Tuscany's classic wines primarily use Sangiovese grapes, the Super Tuscans often include international varietals like Cabernet Sauvignon, Merlot, and Syrah. This innovative approach started in the 1970s when a few pioneering winemakers began experimenting with these grapes, creating rich, full-bodied wines that quickly gained international acclaim.

Bolgheri's landscape contributes greatly to the quality of its wines. The region benefits from a combination of coastal influences and well-drained, sandy soils, which are ideal for growing the international grape varieties used in Super Tuscans. The gentle sea breezes help to moderate temperatures, allowing the grapes to ripen perfectly while retaining their freshness and acidity.

One of the most famous Super Tuscans from Bolgheri is Sassicaia, produced by the Tenuta San Guido estate. Sassicaia is often regarded as one of Italy's finest wines, known for its complex aromas of dark fruit, spices, and cedar, along with its elegant and long-lasting finish. Another well-known label is Ornellaia, which produces a blend of Cabernet Sauvignon, Merlot, and Cabernet Franc, offering a rich, opulent taste with layers of dark fruit and a hint of vanilla.

Visiting Bolgheri provides an opportunity to explore its renowned wineries and taste these exceptional Super Tuscans. Many of the estates offer guided tours where you can learn about their winemaking processes, from vineyard management to aging in oak barrels. These tours often include tastings of their flagship wines, allowing you to experience the full range of flavors and aromas that Bolgheri's Super Tuscans have to offer.

The village of Bolgheri itself is charming and inviting. Its medieval streets are lined with boutiques, cafes, and wine shops where you can sample local wines and enjoy regional specialties. The village is also known for its annual events, such as the "Sagra del Tartufo" (Truffle Festival), which celebrates local truffles and other gourmet foods, creating a lively atmosphere for visitors.

The road leading into Bolgheri, known as the "Cypress Avenue" (Viale dei Cipressi), is particularly striking. Flanked by rows of tall cypress trees, this scenic drive offers a picturesque introduction to the region and its vineyards. It's a popular spot for photos and a beautiful way to appreciate the landscape as you approach the village.

In addition to wine tours and tastings, Bolgheri's surrounding countryside provides opportunities for outdoor activities like hiking and biking. The rolling hills and vineyards create a stunning backdrop for exploring the region's natural beauty.

Bolgheri is a must-visit destination for wine enthusiasts interested in experiencing the innovation and excellence of the Super Tuscans. With its exceptional wines, charming village, and beautiful landscapes, Bolgheri offers a memorable experience that captures the essence of Tuscany's modern winemaking prowess. Whether you're sampling top-tier wines or enjoying the scenic beauty of the region, Bolgheri is a highlight of Tuscan wine country.

CHAPTER 8.
FOOD CULTURE IN TUSCANY

Traditional Tuscan Dishes

Tuscan cuisine is a celebration of simple, yet rich flavors, deeply rooted in the region's agricultural traditions. Each dish reflects the essence of Tuscany's farm-to-table philosophy, where fresh, local ingredients are transformed into hearty and flavorful meals. Here's a look at five traditional Tuscan dishes, along with my revelatory experiences tasting them for the first time and some health tips for those with allergies or dietary restrictions.

First, there's the classic Ribollita, a robust, vegetable-rich soup made from a base of bread and beans. My initial encounter with Ribollita was a revelation. The first spoonful was a comforting blend of hearty beans, kale, and tender vegetables, all melded together by the rich, slightly sour taste of the old bread used in its preparation. The soup is often served with a drizzle of high-quality olive oil, which adds a lush, finishing touch. It's a dish that feels like a warm hug, perfect for the cooler months.

Pici cacio e pepe is another Tuscan delight that stands out. Pici are thick, hand-rolled pasta strands, and when tossed with just a few ingredients—pecorino cheese and black pepper—they become something truly special. When I first tried Pici cacio e pepe, the simplicity was striking. The creamy pecorino cheese blended beautifully with the sharpness of the black pepper, enveloping the pasta in a rich, velvety sauce. It's a prime example of how Tuscany's culinary tradition values simplicity and quality.

Next, there's Bistecca alla Fiorentina, a famed Florentine steak that's as much about tradition as it is about flavor. This massive T-bone steak is seasoned with just salt and pepper and grilled to perfection, often served rare or medium-rare. My first bite of Bistecca alla Fiorentina was unforgettable—the meat was incredibly tender, with a smoky char that paired perfectly with its natural juices. This dish is more than just a meal; it's a celebration of Tuscan grilling traditions and high-quality beef.

The Panzanella salad is a refreshing Tuscan staple that utilizes stale bread. This salad combines chunks of bread with tomatoes, cucumbers, red onions, and basil, all dressed in a tangy vinaigrette. I was pleasantly surprised by how the bread, soaked in the vinaigrette, absorbed all the vibrant flavors of the fresh vegetables. The result was a dish that was both satisfying and light, perfect for a summer day.

Finally, let's talk about Cantucci (or cantuccini), the Tuscan almond biscuits often enjoyed with Vin Santo, a sweet dessert wine. My first taste of Cantucci was a delightful experience—the biscuits were crisp and crumbly, with a subtle almond flavor that was enhanced when dipped into the sweet, rich Vin Santo. This combination is a quintessential Tuscan treat, perfect for ending a meal on a high note.

For those with allergies or dietary restrictions, Tuscan cuisine offers some challenges but also opportunities for adjustments. Here are a few health tips to consider:

1. Gluten Sensitivities: Traditional Tuscan dishes often contain bread or pasta. For those with gluten sensitivities, it's possible to substitute gluten-free bread and pasta. Many restaurants and home kitchens are increasingly offering these alternatives.

2. Dairy Allergies: Many Tuscan dishes, like Pici cacio e pepe and various cheese-based dishes, contain dairy. For dairy allergies, look for recipes or restaurants that use dairy substitutes like almond milk or vegan cheese.

3. Nut Allergies: Cantucci contains almonds, which can be problematic for those with nut allergies. It's advisable to avoid these biscuits or seek out nut-free alternatives.

4. Meat Restrictions: For those who follow vegetarian or vegan diets, dishes like Ribollita and Panzanella are naturally suitable. Just be sure to confirm that no meat-based broth is used in the Ribollita.

Tuscan cuisine, with its rich flavors and traditional recipes, offers an authentic taste of the region's culinary heritage. Whether you're savoring a comforting Ribollita or enjoying the simple elegance of Pici cacio e pepe, each dish is a testament to Tuscany's dedication to high-quality ingredients and time-honored cooking techniques. Adjustments can be made to accommodate dietary needs, ensuring that everyone can experience the joys of Tuscan food.

Olive Oil: The Liquid Gold of Tuscany

Olive oil is often referred to as the "liquid gold" of Tuscany, and for good reason. This golden elixir is not just a staple in Tuscan kitchens but also a symbol of the region's deep connection to its land and traditions.

In Tuscany, olive oil is much more than a cooking ingredient—it's a way of life. The region's warm, sunny climate and rich soil create the perfect conditions for growing olives, and the ancient methods of harvesting and pressing olives are still cherished today.

The process of making Tuscan olive oil starts with the careful picking of olives, usually by hand, to ensure they are not damaged. The olives are then taken to a mill where they are crushed into a paste. This paste is gently pressed to extract the oil, which is then filtered to remove any impurities. The result is a high-quality olive oil that is fresh, fragrant, and full of flavor.

Tuscan olive oil is renowned for its robust flavor and distinct characteristics. It often has a peppery, slightly bitter taste that balances well with its fruity notes. This complexity makes it a versatile ingredient that enhances a wide range of dishes. It can be drizzled over salads, used as a dipping oil for bread, or incorporated into sauces and marinades.

One of the best ways to experience Tuscan olive oil is to visit a local olive oil farm. Many of these farms offer tours where you can learn about the oil-making process, taste different varieties of olive oil, and purchase bottles directly from the source. These visits are a wonderful opportunity to appreciate the craftsmanship and dedication that go into producing each bottle of this liquid gold.

When selecting olive oil, look for extra virgin olive oil, which is the highest quality and comes from the first pressing of the olives. It's important to choose oil that is labeled with its origin to ensure you are getting authentic Tuscan olive oil. Freshness is key, so check for a harvest date on the bottle and choose oils that are less than a year old.

For those who love to cook, having a good bottle of Tuscan olive oil on hand can elevate your dishes to a new level. Whether you're using it to dress a simple salad or to finish a hearty dish, the rich flavor of Tuscan olive oil adds depth and complexity to every bite.

Tuscan olive oil is a true treasure of the region, reflecting its agricultural heritage and culinary traditions. By choosing high-quality extra virgin olive oil and exploring local farms, you can enjoy the full range of flavors and experiences that this remarkable product has to offer.

Where to Eat: From Trattorias to Michelin-Starred Restaurants

When exploring Tuscany and Florence, the culinary scene offers a rich tapestry of flavors and experiences, from traditional trattorias to elegant Michelin-starred establishments. Here's a guide to some of the best places to eat, ensuring you experience the full range of Tuscan cuisine.

Florence:

1. Trattoria ZaZa

Located in Piazza del Mercato Centrale, Trattoria ZaZa is a beloved spot for both locals and tourists. The ambiance is lively and welcoming, with a rustic charm that embodies traditional Florentine dining. The price range is moderate, with appetizers costing around €10-€15, main courses €15-€25, and desserts €5-€10. Don't miss the signature Florentine steak, a tender, juicy cut of beef cooked to perfection and served with a simple yet flavorful seasoning.

2. Osteria Santo Spirito

Nestled in the Santo Spirito neighborhood, this cozy osteria offers a more intimate dining experience. The setting is casual, with a warm, rustic feel that makes it a great spot for a relaxed meal. Prices are reasonable, with appetizers at €8-€12, main courses €12-€20, and desserts €4-€8. The pasta dishes, especially the pici cacio e pepe, are standout choices, showcasing simple ingredients in an extraordinary way.

3. La Giostra

For a touch of elegance, La Giostra offers a refined dining experience in the heart of Florence. The restaurant has a romantic, upscale atmosphere with charming decor and attentive service. Expect to spend about €20-€30 for appetizers, €30-€50 for main courses, and €10-€15 for desserts. The pear and pecorino ravioli is a must-try, celebrated for its delicate balance of sweet and savory flavors.

4. Il Santo Bevitore

This trendy spot in the Oltrarno district combines modern flair with traditional Tuscan ingredients. The ambiance is chic and contemporary, making it a perfect choice for a stylish dinner. Prices are mid-range, with appetizers €12-€18, main courses €18-€30, and desserts €6-€12. The slow-cooked pork belly is a standout dish, renowned for its rich, tender meat and accompanying savory sauces.

5. Michelin-Starred Enoteca Pinchiorri
For a top-tier dining experience, Enoteca Pinchiorri is a three-Michelin-star restaurant offering exceptional gourmet cuisine. The atmosphere is luxurious and sophisticated, ideal for a special occasion. The cost reflects its exclusivity, with tasting menus starting at €200 per person. Signature dishes include the veal with truffle sauce and the impressive wine list that features some of the best Italian and international selections.

Tuscany:

1. La Porta
In the charming hilltop town of Monticchiello, La Porta provides a delightful experience with its rustic, country ambiance. The setting is casual and welcoming, perfect for a leisurely meal. Expect to pay around €10-€15 for appetizers, €20-€30 for main courses, and €5-€10 for desserts. The pici cacio e pepe is a local favorite, with its simple, flavorful combination of cheese and pepper.

2. Osteria del Borgo

Located in the heart of Pienza, this osteria offers traditional Tuscan dishes in a cozy, family-friendly setting. Prices are moderate, with appetizers €8-€12, main courses €15-€25, and desserts €5-€8. The pici with wild boar ragù is highly recommended, showcasing the rich, hearty flavors of Tuscan cuisine.

3. Ristorante La Buca delle Fate

In the beautiful town of San Gimignano, La Buca delle Fate offers a warm, intimate dining atmosphere with a focus on local ingredients. The restaurant's pricing is reasonable, with appetizers around €10-€15, main courses €20-€30, and desserts €5-€10. Try the wild boar stew, a classic Tuscan dish that's both flavorful and comforting.

4. Michelin-Starred La Locanda di Guido

For a refined dining experience in Tuscany, La Locanda di Guido in the town of Montalcino offers a Michelin-starred menu that combines innovation with tradition. The setting is elegant and upscale, making it ideal for a special evening. Expect to spend around €150-€250 per person for a tasting menu. The duck breast with truffle and the locally sourced wines are standout features of the menu.

5. Il Frantoio

In the town of Campiglia Marittima, Il Frantoio is known for its farm-to-table approach and charming, rustic ambiance. The restaurant focuses on fresh, local ingredients, with moderate prices of €15-€20 for appetizers, €25-€35 for main courses, and €8-€12 for desserts. The grilled lamb chops are a highlight, offering a taste of Tuscan authenticity in every bite.

Health Tips for Dietary Restrictions:
When dining in Tuscany and Florence, be mindful of common allergens such as gluten, dairy, and nuts. Many restaurants are accommodating of dietary restrictions, but it's always best to inform the staff of any allergies when you arrive. Tuscan cuisine often includes a variety of vegetables and meats, which can be suitable for those with specific dietary needs. For gluten-free options, ask for dishes made with polenta or rice. If you have dairy allergies, many restaurants can offer alternatives or modifications to their dishes.

Tuscany and Florence offer a rich culinary landscape with diverse dining options, ensuring that every meal is a memorable experience. Whether you're enjoying a casual trattoria or indulging in a Michelin-starred feast, you'll find plenty of opportunities to savor the flavors of this beautiful region.

Tuscan Markets: Fresh Produce and Local Delicacies

Exploring Tuscan markets is a delightful way to experience the region's rich culinary heritage. These markets burst with fresh produce, local delicacies, and an authentic taste of Tuscan life. Here's a guide to some of the best markets in Tuscany where you can immerse yourself in the local flavors and traditions.

In Florence, the Mercato Centrale is a vibrant hub located in the heart of the city. This bustling market offers a wide variety of fresh produce, including ripe tomatoes, crisp greens, and fragrant herbs. As you wander through the aisles, you'll find vendors selling an array of local cheeses, cured meats, and artisanal breads. The upper floor of the market has been transformed into a gourmet food court with stalls offering prepared dishes like fresh pasta and truffle-infused specialties. The atmosphere is lively and perfect for experiencing the essence of Florentine food culture.

Another must-visit market in Florence is the Sant'Ambrogio Market. Located in the historic Sant'Ambrogio district, this market is less touristy than Mercato Centrale and offers a more local vibe. Here, you can shop for seasonal fruits and vegetables, homemade pasta, and freshly baked pastries. The market also features stalls with a variety of Tuscan meats, including juicy sausages and rich salamis, making it a great place to sample traditional flavors.

In Siena, the weekly market held in Piazza del Mercato is a fantastic place to discover local produce and specialties. The market is known for its selection of fresh, high-quality ingredients such as vegetables, cheeses, and olives. Siena's market also offers a range of baked goods and traditional sweets, including the famous panforte, a dense fruitcake packed with nuts and spices. The lively atmosphere and the chance to interact with local vendors add to the charm of this market.

In the charming town of Lucca, the Mercato delle Erbe is a local favorite. Set in a historic building, this market features a variety of fresh produce, including colorful fruits and vegetables, as well as Tuscan staples like olive oil and balsamic vinegar. The market also offers a selection of artisanal cheeses and meats, making it an excellent spot to pick up ingredients for a homemade Tuscan meal. The relaxed, friendly atmosphere of the market reflects the warmth and hospitality of the local community.

In Arezzo, the weekly market in Piazza Grande is another excellent place to explore Tuscan produce. The market is known for its wide range of fresh fruits, vegetables, and local cheeses. You'll also find stalls selling traditional Tuscan products like honey, wine, and handmade pasta. The market's location in the historic heart of Arezzo adds to the experience, allowing you to enjoy the beautiful surroundings while you shop.

Tuscan markets offer a sensory feast, from the vibrant colors of fresh produce to the enticing aromas of local delicacies. Visiting these markets is not only a great way to find high-quality ingredients but also an opportunity to engage with local culture and traditions. Whether you're cooking a meal at home or just enjoying the lively atmosphere, these markets provide a genuine taste of Tuscany.

CHAPTER 9.
EXPERIENCING THE TUSCAN LIFESTYLE

Cultural Etiquette and Language Tips

Understanding cultural etiquette and language tips can greatly enhance your experience in Tuscany and Florence. Here's a simple guide to help you navigate social interactions and communicate effectively during your visit.

When it comes to cultural etiquette, Italians are known for their warm and friendly demeanor. In Tuscany, it's customary to greet people with a polite "buongiorno" (good morning) or "buonasera" (good evening), depending on the time of day. When entering shops or restaurants, a friendly greeting like "ciao" (hi) or "salve" (hello) is appreciated. A smile and a courteous attitude go a long way in creating positive interactions.

In restaurants, it's polite to wait to be seated by the staff rather than choosing your table. When dining, keep in mind that meals in Tuscany are often leisurely affairs, so it's normal for dining experiences to last a few hours. Italians typically have a starter, a pasta or rice dish, a main course, and dessert, and they may enjoy multiple courses over several hours. Tipping is not obligatory, but rounding up the bill or leaving a small amount of change is a nice gesture to show appreciation for good service.

When visiting religious sites such as churches or basilicas, dress modestly. It's respectful to cover your shoulders and avoid wearing hats. Inside these places, speak quietly and turn off your phone to maintain the peaceful atmosphere.

In terms of language, while many people in Tuscany and Florence understand and speak English, learning a few basic Italian phrases can be very helpful and is appreciated by locals. Simple phrases such as "per favore" (please), "grazie" (thank you), and "mi scusi" (excuse me) can make a big difference in your interactions. If you need assistance, you can ask, "Parla inglese?" (Do you speak English?), but try to use Italian phrases whenever possible.

When it comes to ordering food, you might want to familiarize yourself with some common terms. For instance, "un tavolo per due, per favore" means "a table for two, please." If you want to order a specific dish, you can say, "Vorrei ordinare..." followed by the name of the dish. When you're ready to pay, you can ask for the check by saying "Il conto, per favore."

Italians place great importance on politeness and respect, so using "per favore" and "grazie" frequently is a good practice. When interacting with locals, especially in smaller towns, showing an interest in their culture and traditions can lead to more engaging and friendly conversations.

Embracing local customs and making an effort to use the Italian language will enhance your travel experience and help you connect more meaningfully with the people you meet. Remember, a smile and genuine effort go a long way in any culture.

Agriturismos: Staying on Tuscan Farms

Staying at an agriturismo in Tuscany offers a unique and immersive way to experience the region. Agriturismos are working farms that provide accommodations and allow visitors to enjoy a genuine Tuscan countryside experience.

Agriturismos are scattered throughout Tuscany, nestled among rolling hills, vineyards, and olive groves. These charming establishments range from rustic farmhouses to more luxurious lodgings, all offering a chance to connect with the land and its traditions.

When you stay at an agriturismo, you'll find that the atmosphere is often relaxed and welcoming. Many agriturismos are family-run, and the owners are usually eager to share their knowledge about farming, local traditions, and Tuscan cuisine. The accommodations can vary greatly, from simple rooms to spacious apartments or even entire villas, but they all share a common feature: a deep connection to the land and its produce.

One of the highlights of staying at an agriturismo is the chance to enjoy farm-fresh meals. Many agriturismos serve meals made from ingredients grown on the farm, such as vegetables, fruits, meats, and cheeses. These meals are typically hearty and flavorful, reflecting the rich culinary traditions of Tuscany. Breakfasts might include freshly baked bread, homemade jams, and local cheeses, while dinners could feature traditional dishes like ribollita (a hearty vegetable soup) or pici cacio e pepe (thick pasta with cheese and pepper).

In addition to enjoying delicious food, staying at an agriturismo allows you to participate in farm activities.

Depending on the season and the specific farm, you might be able to help with grape harvesting, olive picking, or cheese making. These hands-on experiences provide insight into the daily life of Tuscan farmers and offer a deeper appreciation for the region's agricultural heritage.

The location of an agriturismo is often ideal for exploring the Tuscan countryside. Many are situated close to picturesque towns and villages, making it easy to take day trips and discover local attractions. Whether you're interested in visiting historic sites, wine tasting, or simply enjoying the beautiful landscapes, you'll find plenty to do nearby.

When choosing an agriturismo, consider what kind of experience you're looking for. Some offer a more luxurious stay with amenities like swimming pools and spas, while others focus on providing an authentic farm experience with simple, comfortable accommodations. It's also worth checking if the agriturismo offers cooking classes or tours, which can be a fun way to learn more about Tuscan cuisine.

To book a stay at an agriturismo, look for reputable booking sites or directly visit the farm's website. Reviews from previous guests can offer valuable insights into what to expect. Prices can vary depending on the season, the type of accommodation, and the services offered, so it's a good idea to compare options and plan ahead.

Staying at an agriturismo in Tuscany is a wonderful way to immerse yourself in the region's rural charm and enjoy authentic Tuscan hospitality. Whether you're savoring farm-fresh meals, participating in agricultural activities, or simply relaxing amidst beautiful scenery, an agriturismo stay offers a memorable and enriching travel experience.

Slow Living and Slow Food Movement

The Slow Living and Slow Food movements are all about taking the time to appreciate life's simple pleasures, focusing on quality over speed, and valuing traditions and local resources. These ideas have deep roots in Tuscany and Florence, where the pace of life tends to be more relaxed, and there's a strong connection to local food and culture.

Slow Living is a lifestyle that emphasizes savoring each moment, reducing stress, and prioritizing well-being over the hustle and bustle of modern life. It encourages people to slow down and appreciate life's simple joys, whether that's enjoying a leisurely meal, spending time with family, or simply soaking in the beauty of the surroundings. In Tuscany, this might mean taking a long walk through the countryside, relaxing in a charming village square, or unwinding at a local agriturismo.

The Slow Food movement, founded in Italy in the 1980s, is closely related but focuses specifically on food. It advocates for preserving traditional cooking methods, supporting local farmers and artisans, and enjoying meals that are prepared with care and attention. This movement was born in response to the rise of fast food and the loss of culinary traditions. In Tuscany, it means enjoying dishes made from locally grown ingredients, savoring wines from nearby vineyards, and participating in food festivals that celebrate regional specialties.

In Tuscany and Florence, you can experience the Slow Food movement in various ways. Many restaurants and trattorias emphasize local, seasonal ingredients and traditional cooking methods. They offer dishes that reflect the rich culinary heritage of the region, such as ribollita (a hearty vegetable soup), pici cacio e pepe (thick pasta with cheese and pepper), and delicious, fresh bread.

Local markets are another great place to embrace the Slow Food philosophy. Markets in Tuscany are filled with fresh produce, cheeses, meats, and other local delicacies. Shopping at these markets not only supports local farmers and producers but also allows you to enjoy ingredients that are at their peak of flavor.

Participating in a traditional Tuscan meal is an excellent way to experience the Slow Food movement. Meals are often leisurely affairs, starting with antipasti (appetizers) and moving on to pasta, main courses, and desserts, all enjoyed at a relaxed pace. Many restaurants and agriturismos take pride in preparing meals from scratch and using ingredients sourced from their own farms or nearby producers.

If you're interested in the Slow Living lifestyle, consider staying in an agriturismo or choosing accommodations that emphasize relaxation and connection with nature. Engage in activities that allow you to slow down and appreciate the region's beauty, like hiking through the hills, visiting local vineyards, or exploring charming towns.

The Slow Living and Slow Food movements in Tuscany and Florence offer a refreshing contrast to the fast-paced nature of modern life. They encourage you to savor each moment, enjoy high-quality food, and support local traditions. Embracing these principles can lead to a more fulfilling and memorable travel experience, allowing you to connect deeply with the region's culture and way of life.

Festivals and Traditions

Palio di Siena

I had always been intrigued by the Palio di Siena, the famous horse race held twice a year in Siena. The vibrant images I had seen online – the colorful districts racing around the Piazza del Campo – had always captured my imagination. So, when I found myself in Siena during the summer, I knew I had to see it for myself.

The city buzzed with excitement in the days leading up to the race. Each district, or contrada, was busy getting their horses and jockeys ready, and the streets were alive with people wearing their contrada's colors. I managed to get a spot in the grandstand, and as the race began, the noise from the crowd was incredible.

The horses sped around the square, and their jockeys expertly handled them through the tight turns. The competition was intense, and everyone in the crowd was on edge. Sitting near some locals, I couldn't help but be swept up in their enthusiasm.

"This is the most thrilling event in Siena," one local told me. "It's a tradition that has been around for centuries, and it's something we're all very proud of."

I couldn't agree more. The Palio was more than just a horse race; it was a celebration of Siena's rich history and culture. As the winning horse crossed the finish line, the crowd erupted in cheers. The winning contrada would enjoy bragging rights for the next year, and their victory would be celebrated throughout the city.

Leaving the Piazza del Campo, I felt a deep sense of awe. The Palio di Siena was a truly unique and memorable experience. It reminded me of the deep passion and tradition that continue to thrive in this historic Tuscan city.

Artisanal Crafts: Pottery, Leatherwork, and Textiles

In Tuscany, the tradition of artisanal crafts is alive and vibrant, with skilled artisans creating beautiful pottery, leatherwork, and textiles that reflect the region's rich history and culture.

When it comes to pottery, Tuscany is renowned for its exquisite pieces. Local potters often use traditional methods passed down through generations to create handcrafted ceramics. You'll find a range of pottery styles, from delicate, colorful tiles to sturdy, rustic vases. Many of these pieces are decorated with intricate patterns inspired by Tuscan landscapes and historical motifs. Visiting a pottery workshop can be a wonderful way to see the craft in action and perhaps pick up a unique souvenir. In cities like Florence and Siena, you can find local shops showcasing these beautiful items, where each piece tells a story of Tuscan artistry.

Leatherwork is another treasured craft in Tuscany. The region is famous for its high-quality leather goods, including bags, belts, and shoes. Artisans here use time-honored techniques to create leather products that are both stylish and durable. The leather is often dyed in rich, natural colors and can be customized to fit individual tastes. Florence is particularly well-known for its leather markets, where you can find everything from luxurious handbags to practical travel accessories. The quality of Tuscan leather is exceptional, and purchasing a handcrafted leather item can be a special way to remember your visit.

Textiles are also a significant part of Tuscany's artisanal heritage. From woven fabrics to hand-stitched linens, the craftsmanship in textiles is remarkable. Tuscan textiles often feature traditional patterns and high-quality materials, including linen and wool. You might find beautiful hand-woven scarves, embroidered tablecloths, and other items that showcase the skill and creativity of local artisans. In towns like Prato, which is known for its textile industry, you can explore workshops and boutiques offering a range of beautifully crafted textile goods.

Experiencing these artisanal crafts firsthand can be incredibly rewarding. Each piece you see is a testament to the dedication and expertise of its maker. Whether you're exploring a pottery studio, browsing leather shops, or admiring textile creations, you'll gain a deeper appreciation for the artistry that defines Tuscany. If you have the chance, visiting these workshops or markets will not only give you a glimpse into local craftsmanship but also allow you to take home a piece of Tuscany's rich artisanal tradition.

Sustainable Travel: Eco-Friendly Options

Traveling sustainably in Tuscany is a wonderful way to enjoy the region's beauty while minimizing your impact on the environment. Here's how you can make eco-friendly choices during your visit.

Start by considering transportation options that are kinder to the environment. Instead of renting a car, which can contribute to pollution, opt for trains or buses. Tuscany has a good network of trains connecting cities and towns, making it easy to travel without a car. Many train services are efficient and comfortable, and they allow you to enjoy the scenery without the stress of driving. Buses are also a great option for shorter trips and are often an affordable choice.

If you prefer to explore the Tuscan countryside, look into bike rentals. Many cities, including Florence and Siena, offer bike rental services. Cycling is not only an eco-friendly way to travel but also gives you a chance to see the landscape up close. There are also bike paths and scenic routes that make biking a pleasant and rewarding experience.

When it comes to accommodation, choosing eco-friendly lodging is a fantastic way to support sustainable travel. Many hotels and guesthouses in Tuscany are committed to green practices. Look for places that have received eco-certifications or are known for their efforts in reducing waste and conserving energy. Some hotels use solar power, recycle waste, and support local communities. Staying in these accommodations ensures that your travel choices contribute positively to the environment.

Dining sustainably is another important aspect. Tuscany is known for its farm-to-table restaurants, which source ingredients locally and support local farmers. Eating at these establishments not only provides you with fresh, delicious food but also reduces the carbon footprint associated with long-distance food transportation. Additionally, many restaurants focus on using seasonal ingredients, which are better for the environment.

When shopping for souvenirs, consider items that are locally made and crafted sustainably. Tuscany is known for its artisanal products, such as pottery and textiles. Purchasing these items supports local artisans and helps reduce the environmental impact of mass-produced goods. Be mindful of plastic use and opt for products that are packaged in eco-friendly materials.

Lastly, respect the natural environment during your visit. Follow local guidelines for waste disposal, avoid littering, and stick to marked trails when hiking. By being considerate of the environment, you help preserve Tuscany's natural beauty for future travelers to enjoy.

Incorporating these sustainable practices into your travel plans allows you to experience Tuscany's charm while contributing to its preservation. Each small effort adds up, making a big difference in protecting the environment and supporting local communities.

CHAPTER 10.
OUTDOOR ACTIVITIES

Hiking Trails and Nature Reserves

Hiking in Tuscany offers the perfect blend of nature, history, and breathtaking landscapes. The region is full of trails and nature reserves where you can enjoy the rolling hills, forests, and vineyards that make Tuscany so famous. Whether you're an experienced hiker or just looking for a peaceful walk in the countryside, there's something for everyone.

One of the most beautiful places to hike is the Via Francigena, an ancient pilgrimage route that stretches across Europe. In Tuscany, this trail takes you through medieval towns like San Gimignano, Monteriggioni, and Siena. Walking along this historic path feels like stepping back in time, surrounded by vineyards, olive groves, and cypress trees. You'll also pass by small villages where you can stop for a glass of local wine or a meal. The trail is easy to follow, with signposts along the way, and there are shorter sections you can hike if you're not up for the entire route. To get to the trail, it depends on which section you want to start from. For example, you can take a bus or train to San Gimignano or Siena, and start your hike from there.

Another stunning area to explore is the Casentino Forest National Park, located in the northern part of Tuscany. It's one of Italy's largest forests and is home to deer, wild boar, and a variety of bird species. The park has numerous trails, ranging from easy walks to more challenging hikes. One of the most popular routes takes you to the Sanctuary of La Verna, a peaceful and spiritual place where St. Francis of Assisi once lived. Hiking through the dense woods, you'll feel a deep connection with nature. There are also waterfalls, streams, and stunning panoramic views along the trails. To get there, you can take a train to the town of Stia, which is near the park, and then either hike or drive to one of the many trailheads.

For those who prefer a coastal experience, the Maremma Regional Park is the ideal spot. Located along the southern Tuscan coast, this nature reserve is known for its rugged cliffs, sandy beaches, and wild landscapes. The park is less crowded than other tourist areas, making it a peaceful escape. There are several trails you can follow, including one that leads to the stunning Cala di Forno beach, a secluded paradise with crystal-clear waters. The wildlife here is also amazing – you might spot wild horses, foxes, and various bird species. To enjoy your time fully, pack a picnic and spend the day relaxing on the beach or hiking through the coastal hills. The park is accessible by car, and the nearest town is Alberese, which is a short drive from the entrance of the park.

Closer to Florence, you can explore Monte Morello, a mountain that offers incredible views of the city and the surrounding countryside. The hiking trails here vary in difficulty, so you can choose a shorter, easier walk or challenge yourself with a longer hike to the top. The peak of Monte Morello offers panoramic views all the way to the Apennine Mountains. The fresh air and natural surroundings make it a great escape from the hustle and bustle of Florence. To get there, you can take a bus from Florence to Sesto Fiorentino, and from there, it's a short drive or hike to the trailheads.

Lastly, for a true hidden gem, head to the Apuan Alps. This mountain range, located in northern Tuscany, is famous for its marble quarries, but it's also a fantastic spot for hiking. The trails here are more challenging, with steep climbs and rocky terrain, but the views from the top are worth the effort. One of the best hikes is to Monte Forato, a peak with a natural arch carved into the rock. From the summit, you can see both the Tuscan countryside and the coast. It's a bit off the beaten path, so it's perfect for those looking for a quieter, more adventurous experience. To get there, you can drive to the town of Fornovolasco, where several trails start.

No matter where you choose to hike in Tuscany, be sure to bring plenty of water, sunscreen, and good walking shoes. The trails can be hot in the summer, but the views and experiences you'll gain along the way make it all worthwhile. Every hike offers something special, whether it's the chance to see wildlife, discover hidden villages, or simply enjoy the incredible natural beauty of Tuscany.

Biking Through the Vineyards and Countryside

Biking through the vineyards and countryside of Tuscany is one of the most delightful ways to experience the region. The gentle hills, lined with vineyards, olive groves, and cypress trees, make for a scenic and peaceful ride. Whether you're an avid cyclist or just enjoy a leisurely bike ride, the roads and paths of Tuscany offer routes for every skill level.

One of the most popular areas to bike in Tuscany is the Chianti region, which lies between Florence and Siena. The landscape here is picture-perfect, with rolling hills, vineyards, and small villages dotted along the way. Many visitors choose to start their ride from Greve in Chianti, a charming town known for its wine and local products. You can rent a bike in the town and start your journey from there. As you ride, you'll pass vineyards and wineries where you can stop for tastings or just enjoy the beautiful views. The quiet country roads are perfect for biking, and you'll often find yourself alone with the scenery, far from the busy tourist spots.

Another great biking route is the road from San Gimignano to Volterra. San Gimignano is known for its medieval towers, and starting your ride here offers a great mix of history and nature. The road between these two towns is a bit more challenging with steeper hills, but the effort is worth it. Along the way, you'll pass vineyards, olive groves, and panoramic views of the surrounding countryside. Volterra itself is a wonderful reward at the end of your ride, a town rich in Etruscan history and charming streets to explore. To get there, you can take a train or bus from Florence to Poggibonsi, and from there, it's a short bus ride to San Gimignano, where you can rent a bike or join a guided tour.

If you prefer a coastal experience, the Maremma region in southern Tuscany offers a different kind of beauty. This area is less touristy, and the roads are quiet and perfect for biking. You can ride through the Maremma Regional Park, where you'll see wild horses, foxes, and lush, unspoiled landscapes. The trails here take you through vineyards, past ancient farmhouses, and down to the coast, where you can enjoy a swim in the sea after a long ride. The nearby town of Alberese is a good starting point, and you can rent a bike there or even join a guided tour that takes you through the best parts of the park. To get there, take a train to Grosseto, then a bus to Alberese, which is just a short distance from the park entrance.

For those who want a more leisurely ride, the Val d'Orcia offers some of the most iconic Tuscan landscapes. This region, with its soft, rolling hills and golden fields, is perfect for a relaxing bike ride. Start your journey in Pienza, a small Renaissance town known for its stunning views of the countryside. From Pienza, you can ride towards Montepulciano, passing through vineyards and farms along the way. The roads here are gentle, and the scenery is straight out of a postcard. Montepulciano itself is famous for its Vino Nobile wine, so make sure to stop for a tasting at one of the local wineries before heading back. Pienza is accessible by bus from Siena, and bike rentals are available in town.

For an adventurous ride, head to the Apuan Alps. This mountain range in northern Tuscany offers a more rugged landscape, with steep climbs and challenging routes. One of the best rides is to the town of Carrara, famous for its marble quarries. The ride is more intense than other routes in Tuscany, with sharp turns and steep inclines, but the views of the mountains and the sea in the distance are worth the effort. Carrara can be reached by train from Florence or Pisa, and you can rent bikes locally or bring your own if you prefer.

To make the most of your biking experience in Tuscany, I recommend planning your route in advance and checking the weather before you go. Bring plenty of water, especially if you're biking in the summer, and pack a light lunch to enjoy along the way. There are many small picnic spots where you can stop and take in the views. Whether you prefer a relaxing ride through vineyards or a challenging mountain climb, biking through Tuscany offers a unique and unforgettable way to experience this beautiful region.

Hot Springs and Spas

Tuscany is not just about rolling hills and vineyards; it's also home to some of Italy's most incredible hot springs and spas. These natural thermal waters have been used for centuries to heal, relax, and rejuvenate, and they offer a wonderful way to unwind in the heart of the Tuscan countryside. Whether you're looking for a luxurious spa experience or a rustic soak in a natural pool, Tuscany has something to offer.

One of the most famous hot springs in Tuscany is Saturnia, located in the southern part of the region, near the town of Manciano. The hot springs here are well-known for their warm, sulfur-rich waters that flow naturally from the ground at a constant temperature of about 37°C (98°F). The thermal waterfalls, known as Cascate del Mulino, are free to the public and offer an unforgettable experience. The water cascades into natural pools formed by limestone, and you can sit and soak while surrounded by the beautiful Tuscan landscape. Getting there is easy by car; Saturnia is about a two-hour drive from Florence, and there's plenty of parking nearby. Bring a towel and be prepared to relax in the warm water for hours.

If you're looking for a more luxurious experience, head to Bagno Vignoni, a charming village in the Val d'Orcia. This tiny village has been famous for its thermal waters since Roman times, and today it offers both public and private hot springs. The main square, Piazza delle Sorgenti, is unique because it features a large pool of steaming thermal water right in the middle of town. While you can't bathe in this central pool, there are several nearby hotels and spas where you can enjoy the waters. The Adler Spa Resort in Bagno Vignoni is particularly popular, offering thermal pools, wellness treatments, and stunning views of the surrounding countryside. If you don't mind spending a little extra, this is the perfect place to indulge in some serious relaxation.

For a more rustic and natural experience, check out Bagni San Filippo, located near the town of Castiglione d'Orcia. These hot springs are nestled in a forest, and the atmosphere is peaceful and quiet. The thermal water here flows over white limestone formations, creating a stunning backdrop for your soak. One of the most famous formations is called the White Whale, a massive rock covered in white mineral deposits from the thermal water. The hot springs here are free to the public, and there's no need to book ahead. You can simply walk into the forest, find a spot in one of the natural pools, and enjoy the warm water. It's about a 30-minute drive from Montepulciano, and there is parking nearby, but it's best to wear sturdy shoes as you'll need to walk a short distance through the woods to reach the springs.

Another great spot to visit is Rapolano Terme, located in the Crete Senesi area, not far from Siena. This small town is home to several thermal spas, including the Terme Antica Querciolaia and Terme San Giovanni, both of which offer a range of thermal pools and wellness treatments. The water in Rapolano is known for its high mineral content, which is said to help with skin conditions, joint pain, and muscle tension. The spas here are perfect for a day of pampering, with indoor and outdoor pools, saunas, and massage treatments. The atmosphere is relaxing, and you can easily spend a full day enjoying the water and the peaceful surroundings. Rapolano

Terme is easy to reach by car from Siena, and there are buses that run regularly from the city if you prefer not to drive.

Lastly, for a truly off-the-beaten-path experience, visit Petriolo, located in the Maremma region. These hot springs are less touristy and offer a more rugged, natural experience. The water here is rich in sulfur and flows into the Farma River, where you can enjoy both hot and cold water depending on where you sit. There's a mix of public and private areas, so if you're looking for a free soak, head to the natural pools along the riverbank. If you want a more structured experience, there's also a hotel with thermal pools and spa services nearby. Petriolo is about an hour's drive from Siena, and the best way to get there is by car, as it's located in a more remote part of Tuscany.

Whichever hot spring or spa you choose, spending time in these thermal waters is a perfect way to unwind and connect with the natural beauty of Tuscany. Remember to bring a towel, some water shoes, and a relaxed mindset as you prepare to soak in Tuscany's natural hot springs. It's an experience you won't soon forget!

The Tuscan Archipelago: Islands of Elba and Giglio

The Tuscan Archipelago is a hidden gem in Italy, made up of several beautiful islands, with Elba and Giglio being the most well-known. These islands are perfect for anyone looking for stunning landscapes, crystal-clear waters, and a peaceful escape from the mainland. Each island has its own unique charm, offering visitors the chance to explore their natural beauty, rich history, and vibrant local culture.

Elba, the largest island in the Tuscan Archipelago, is perhaps most famous as the place where Napoleon Bonaparte was exiled in 1814. But beyond its historical significance, Elba is a paradise for nature lovers. The island is covered in lush green hills, with small villages scattered throughout, and its coastline is dotted with pristine beaches. You can visit Portoferraio, the island's main town, which has a picturesque harbor and a well-preserved old town. Here, you can explore Napoleon's residence, visit the Medici Fortress, or simply enjoy a meal at one of the many seaside restaurants offering fresh seafood and local dishes.

For beach lovers, Elba offers a variety of options. Spiaggia di Sansone is one of the most beautiful beaches on the island, with its white pebbles and turquoise waters perfect for swimming and snorkeling. If you're looking for a quieter spot, head to Cavoli Beach on the southern coast, which is known for its calm waters and relaxed atmosphere. For those who love hiking, the island has several trails, including the hike up to Monte Capanne, the highest peak on Elba. From the top, you'll get a breathtaking view of the entire island and the surrounding sea.

To get to Elba, you can take a ferry from Piombino, a port town on the mainland. The ferry ride takes about an hour, and once you arrive, it's easy to rent a car or scooter to explore the island at your own pace. If you prefer not to drive, buses and taxis are available as well.

While Elba is the largest island, Giglio is much smaller but just as beautiful. Located closer to the mainland, Giglio is a haven for those looking for crystal-clear waters and unspoiled natural landscapes. The main town, Giglio Porto, is a charming fishing village with pastel-colored houses lining the waterfront. It's a great place to enjoy fresh seafood and watch the boats come and go. The island's second town, Giglio Castello, is perched high on a hill and offers panoramic views of the surrounding sea. The narrow, cobblestone streets and medieval architecture make it feel like stepping back in time.

Giglio is perfect for outdoor activities. Caldane Beach is one of the island's most famous beaches, known for its crystal-clear water and peaceful setting. It's a bit of a hike to get there, but once you arrive, you'll feel like you've found a hidden paradise. For snorkeling and diving enthusiasts, Campese Bay offers incredible underwater views, with colorful marine life and rocky reefs to explore. If you enjoy hiking, there are several trails that wind through the island's hills, offering spectacular views along the way.

To reach Giglio, you can take a ferry from Porto Santo Stefano, a coastal town on the mainland. The ferry ride is short, about an hour, making Giglio an easy day trip if you're staying nearby. Once on the island, you can explore on foot, by bike, or by taking one of the local buses.

Both Elba and Giglio offer a unique and peaceful escape from the busier parts of Tuscany. Whether you're interested in history, outdoor activities, or simply relaxing by the sea, these islands are the perfect destination for an unforgettable Tuscan adventure. Be sure to plan ahead, especially in the summer months, when these islands become popular with both locals and tourists looking for a serene retreat.

CHAPTER 11.
DAY TRIPS FROM FLORENCE

Fiesole: Ancient History and Spectacular Views

Fiesole is a small town perched on a hilltop just a short distance from Florence, offering a peaceful escape with stunning views and a rich history that dates back to ancient times. The town is less crowded than Florence, making it a perfect place to relax while still being immersed in Tuscany's culture and history.

Fiesole's history goes all the way back to the Etruscans, who founded the town around the 8th century BC, long before the Romans arrived. You can still see traces of this ancient past when you visit the Archaeological Area. This site contains the remains of an Etruscan temple and city walls, alongside a well-preserved Roman theater and baths. Walking through this area gives you a real sense of what life was like thousands of years ago. The Roman theater is especially impressive, and in the summer, it sometimes hosts outdoor performances, adding a special touch to your visit.

One of the best things about Fiesole is the incredible view it offers of Florence and the surrounding countryside. The view from Piazza Mino, the town's main square, is already impressive, but for an even better view, you can hike up to the San Francesco Monastery. The walk is a bit steep, but the panoramic view from the top is absolutely worth it. From here, you can see Florence's iconic dome and the rolling Tuscan hills stretching out into the distance. The monastery itself is also charming, with a peaceful atmosphere and a small museum.

If you're interested in art and history, the Museo Bandini is another highlight of Fiesole. It's a small museum but houses a beautiful collection of medieval and Renaissance art. The Cathedral of Fiesole (Cattedrale di San Romolo) is also worth a visit. It's a simple but elegant church with a history that stretches back to the 11th century, and it offers a calm spot to rest and reflect.

For nature lovers, Fiesole is surrounded by beautiful walking trails that take you through olive groves, vineyards, and wooded hills. These trails are a great way to explore the Tuscan countryside, and they offer a peaceful contrast to the busy streets of Florence.

Getting to Fiesole is easy. You can take a bus from Florence's Piazza San Marco, and within 20 minutes, you'll find yourself in this charming hilltop town. The bus ride itself offers lovely views as you climb higher into the hills. Once you arrive, you can explore Fiesole on foot since the town is small and easy to navigate.

When you're ready for a break, Fiesole has several cozy cafes and restaurants where you can enjoy a coffee, a glass of local wine, or a traditional Tuscan meal. The peaceful atmosphere and fresh air make dining here a relaxing experience, especially after a day of exploring.

Overall, Fiesole offers a perfect blend of ancient history, stunning views, and a quiet atmosphere, making it an ideal day trip from Florence. Whether you're interested in archaeology, art, nature, or just a peaceful escape, Fiesole is a destination that shouldn't be missed.

Vinci: The Birthplace of Leonardo

Vinci, a small town in the heart of Tuscany, is famous for being the birthplace of one of the world's greatest minds—Leonardo da Vinci. Located just a short drive from Florence, Vinci offers a glimpse into the life and legacy of the man behind masterpieces like the Mona Lisa and The Last Supper. The town itself is charming, with its peaceful streets, olive groves, and vineyards surrounding it.

The main attraction in Vinci is the Museo Leonardiano, a museum dedicated to Leonardo's incredible inventions, studies, and drawings. The museum is housed in two buildings: the Castello dei Conti Guidi and the nearby Palazzina Uzielli. Inside, you'll find models of Leonardo's designs for everything from flying machines to military devices. It's fascinating to see how far ahead of his time he was, with ideas that laid the foundation for many modern inventions. There's also a focus on his scientific studies, showing his diverse interests in anatomy, engineering, and physics.

One of the highlights of visiting Vinci is the opportunity to explore Leonardo's birthplace, known as the Casa Natale di Leonardo. This modest farmhouse, located a short drive from the town center, offers a quiet and reflective atmosphere. While the house itself is simple, it's moving to stand in the place where Leonardo was born in 1452 and to imagine how the natural beauty of the Tuscan countryside may have inspired his genius.

From Vinci, you can also enjoy a beautiful walk or drive through the surrounding hills. The countryside here is quintessentially Tuscan, with its rolling hills, cypress trees, and fields of olive trees and grapevines. The walk between Vinci and Leonardo's birthplace is particularly scenic, offering lovely views of the landscape.

For art lovers, a visit to the Church of Santa Croce in Vinci is a must. Inside, you'll find a small but touching tribute to Leonardo, including a font where it's believed he was baptized. The church itself is simple yet peaceful, with a sense of history that adds to the experience.

Vinci is easy to reach from Florence or Pisa by car, but there are also buses that can take you to this picturesque town. Once there, everything is easily walkable, and you can explore the town's museums, sights, and countryside at a leisurely pace.

When it comes to dining, Vinci offers a few traditional Tuscan restaurants where you can enjoy local dishes like ribollita (Tuscan bread soup) and bistecca alla fiorentina (Florentine steak). After a day of exploring, sitting down to a hearty Tuscan meal with a glass of local wine is the perfect way to relax.

In Vinci, you not only learn about the extraordinary mind of Leonardo da Vinci, but you also get to enjoy the beauty and tranquility of Tuscany. Whether you're a history buff, an art enthusiast, or simply someone who loves exploring charming Italian towns, Vinci is a place that leaves a lasting impression.

Prato: Textiles and Contemporary Art

Prato, located just a short distance from Florence, is a city that blends its rich history in textiles with a modern love for contemporary art. While it might not be as well-known as some of Tuscany's other cities, Prato offers a unique experience for visitors, especially those interested in the fashion and art worlds.

Prato has long been famous for its textile industry, and this heritage is still very much alive today. The Museo del Tessuto (Textile Museum) is the best place to explore this aspect of the city. Located in an old textile mill, the museum showcases the history of fabric production in Prato, from ancient times to modern fashion. It's fascinating to see how textiles have evolved over the centuries and the important role Prato played in the industry. You can see antique fabrics, learn about the weaving process, and admire designs that have influenced fashion around the world.

In addition to its textile history, Prato is home to some striking examples of contemporary art. The Centro per l'Arte Contemporanea Luigi Pecci is one of Italy's top museums for modern art. This futuristic-looking building stands out against the backdrop of Prato's more traditional architecture. Inside, you'll find rotating exhibitions featuring works from both Italian and international artists, as well as a focus on avant-garde and experimental art forms. It's the perfect place to dive into the world of contemporary art, with installations, videos, and multimedia pieces that will leave you thinking long after your visit.

Wandering through Prato's historic center, you'll find it's not all about art and textiles. The city is home to some stunning historical sites as well. The Castello dell'Imperatore is an imposing medieval fortress that was once part of Prato's defense system. Walking through its massive stone walls and climbing up to the top provides great views over the city.

Another must-visit in Prato is the Duomo di Prato (Prato Cathedral), known for its beautiful frescoes by the Renaissance artist Filippo Lippi. The cathedral's exterior may seem simple, but inside you'll discover incredible works of art that tell religious stories in vivid detail. Lippi's frescoes are particularly impressive and are a highlight for anyone interested in Renaissance art.

For those who enjoy Italian cuisine, Prato has its own specialties. The most famous local treat is cantucci, a type of almond biscotti often enjoyed with a glass of Vin Santo, a sweet dessert wine. You can find cantucci in most bakeries and restaurants in Prato, and it's the perfect way to end a meal.

Prato is easily accessible from Florence by train, with the journey taking around 30 minutes. Once in Prato, the city is very walkable, allowing you to explore its charming streets, museums, and historical sites at your own pace.

Prato might not be as famous as Florence or Pisa, but its combination of textile history, contemporary art, and medieval architecture makes it a city worth visiting. Whether you're drawn by its artistic side or its rich industrial past, Prato offers a refreshing break from Tuscany's more crowded tourist spots. It's a city that celebrates both the old and the new, and that's what makes it so special.

CHAPTER 12.
TUSCANY FOR FAMILY

Kid-Friendly Attractions

Tuscany offers a wealth of kid-friendly attractions that make it a great destination for families. Whether your little ones love history, nature, or adventure, there's something for everyone to enjoy.

One of the best places to start is Pinocchio Park in Collodi, the town where the author of Pinocchio, Carlo Collodi, was born. This whimsical park is dedicated to the famous wooden puppet and is filled with playful sculptures, fun trails, and storytelling corners. Children can explore the beautiful gardens, see giant versions of their favorite characters, and enjoy the small rides and puppet shows. The park is more of an outdoor art exhibit than a typical amusement park, making it a charming and peaceful place to explore as a family.

For kids who love animals, the Pistoia Zoo is a wonderful option. Located just outside the city of Pistoia, this zoo is home to over 400 animals from all over the world. Children can see lions, giraffes, and elephants up close, and there are also interactive areas where they can learn more about wildlife and conservation. The zoo is well laid out, making it easy for families to navigate, and it offers picnic areas where you can relax and enjoy a family meal.

In Florence, the Galileo Museum (Museo Galileo) is a fantastic place for curious kids interested in science and history. The museum showcases a wide range of scientific instruments, including telescopes, globes, and clocks that date back centuries. Children can learn about the history of astronomy, physics, and navigation in a fun and interactive way. There are hands-on exhibits and activities that allow kids to get involved in scientific experiments, making it an educational and exciting experience.

For families who enjoy being outdoors, a visit to the Boboli Gardens in Florence is a must. These sprawling gardens are part of the Pitti Palace and provide a beautiful place for kids to run around and explore. The gardens are full of fountains, statues, and hidden pathways, giving children plenty of space to roam and discover new things. Parents can enjoy the stunning views of Florence from the garden's terraces, while kids will love the sense of adventure that comes with wandering through this historic park.

Another great outdoor spot for families is the Cavallino Matto amusement park located along the Tuscan coast in Marina di Castagneto. This theme park offers a variety of rides for kids of all ages, from gentle carousels and mini roller coasters for the little ones to more thrilling rides for older children. The park also has live shows and a large picnic area, making it an ideal spot for a day of family fun.

For a more educational outing, the Museo Leonardo da Vinci in Vinci offers interactive exhibits dedicated to the famous inventor. Kids can see models of Leonardo's inventions and learn about his work as an engineer and artist. The museum makes learning about history and science exciting, and children will leave with a greater appreciation for one of Italy's greatest minds.

Tuscany also has many beaches that are perfect for families. Along the coast, you'll find kid-friendly beaches like Marina di Grosseto and Viareggio, where the waters are shallow and calm. These beaches offer plenty of space for kids to play in the sand, build sandcastles, and paddle in the water. Many of the beaches have facilities like playgrounds and cafés, making it easy for parents to relax while the kids have fun.

Tuscany is a fantastic destination for families, offering a mix of history, culture, and outdoor adventures. Whether your kids love exploring ancient castles, learning about science, or playing on the beach, you'll find plenty to keep them entertained. The region's natural beauty and welcoming atmosphere make it a perfect place to create lasting memories with your family.

Best Activities for Families: Castles, Farms, and Parks

Tuscany is an excellent place for families, with activities that everyone can enjoy. Whether it's exploring old castles, visiting working farms, or spending time in beautiful parks, the region has plenty of family-friendly adventures.

One of the top attractions for families in Tuscany is visiting the many castles scattered across the countryside. Castello di Brolio, located in the heart of the Chianti region, is an excellent choice for families. The castle offers guided tours where you can learn about its history, and children will love imagining themselves as knights and princesses while exploring the ancient walls. The surrounding gardens are perfect for a family stroll, and you can even have a picnic with a stunning view of the Tuscan hills. Many castles also have vineyards, allowing parents to enjoy a bit of local wine while the kids run around the grounds.

Another great activity for families is visiting a farm or staying at an agriturismo (a farm stay). These farms often welcome visitors to learn about traditional Tuscan farming methods, interact with animals, and even participate in activities like olive picking or making fresh pasta. Fattoria di Maiano, near Florence, is a popular choice. This farm has plenty of animals for kids to see, including donkeys, goats, and peacocks, and offers tractor rides and nature walks. Families can also enjoy meals made from fresh, local ingredients at the farm's restaurant, giving everyone a taste of authentic Tuscan cuisine.

For a more hands-on experience, you can visit Petrognano Farm, located near Vinci, where children can try their hand at feeding farm animals and see how a real working farm operates. It's a great way to introduce kids to rural life and let them experience the beauty of the Tuscan countryside.

If your family enjoys spending time outdoors, Tuscany has many beautiful parks that are perfect for a day of exploration. One of the best is Parco delle Cascine in Florence. This large park offers open green spaces for picnics, walking paths, and even playgrounds where children can play. You can rent bikes to explore the park's many trails, or simply relax by the Arno River and enjoy a peaceful afternoon.

For families who love nature, the Tuscan Archipelago National Park is a fantastic place to visit. This park includes several islands off the coast of Tuscany, each with its own unique charm. Families can explore the beaches, take boat tours to see marine life, or hike along scenic trails with beautiful views of the sea. Elba Island, one of the largest in the archipelago, is particularly popular for families because of its beautiful beaches and gentle hiking trails.

In the town of Lucca, you'll find Le Mura di Lucca, the ancient city walls that surround the old town. These walls have been transformed into a park where families can walk or cycle around the perimeter of the town. It's an easy and enjoyable way to see the sights of Lucca, and the kids will love riding bikes along the flat, tree-lined paths. Afterward, you can explore the charming town, with its narrow streets, old churches, and lively squares.

For a fun mix of nature and history, head to the Parco di Pinocchio in Collodi, a theme park dedicated to the famous wooden puppet. This park brings the story of Pinocchio to life with sculptures, interactive exhibits, and outdoor trails. It's an enchanting place for children, who can follow Pinocchio's adventures through the park, while parents will appreciate the peaceful atmosphere and scenic gardens.

Tuscany also has plenty of smaller, local parks that are perfect for a break from sightseeing. Boboli Gardens in Florence is one such spot, with wide paths, fountains, and statues that create a sense of wonder for kids and adults alike. Families can spend hours exploring the different corners of this historic garden, finding hidden statues and enjoying views over the city.

Overall, Tuscany offers a wide range of activities for families, from exploring ancient castles to enjoying the fresh air in beautiful parks. Whether you prefer learning about history, experiencing rural life on a farm, or just enjoying the great outdoors, there's something for everyone to love in this beautiful region.

Planning a Family Itinerary in Tuscany

Planning a family itinerary in Tuscany can be a lot of fun, as the region is filled with activities that suit all ages. Whether your family enjoys history, outdoor adventures, or simply relaxing in beautiful surroundings, Tuscany has plenty to offer.

To start, it's best to divide your time between city exploration and countryside relaxation. A good first stop is Florence, the heart of Tuscany and a city filled with history and culture. Spend a couple of days here visiting places that will interest both adults and children. The Uffizi Gallery and Accademia offer a chance to see masterpieces like Botticelli's "The Birth of Venus" and Michelangelo's "David," while the Boboli Gardens give kids space to run around and explore. Florence is also a very walkable city, so strolling along the Ponte Vecchio or through Piazza della Signoria is easy and enjoyable for everyone.

After spending time in Florence, head to the countryside. The Chianti region is perfect for families who want to experience rural Tuscany. Consider staying in an agriturismo, a farm stay that offers family-friendly accommodations in beautiful surroundings. Many agriturismos, such as Fattoria Poggio Alloro, allow kids to interact with animals, learn about farming, and even try activities like making pasta or helping harvest vegetables. You can also take short day trips to nearby villages like Greve in Chianti or Radda in Chianti, where you can wander through markets and enjoy local food.

For a mix of nature and history, a stop in Lucca is a must. The city is famous for its well-preserved Renaissance walls, which have been turned into a park. Families can rent bikes and ride around the city atop these walls, offering a unique way to explore. Inside the walls, Lucca's narrow streets are lined with cafes and shops, and there are plenty of opportunities to try local gelato or stop for a pizza. This charming town is easy to navigate and perfect for a relaxed family day.

Another family-friendly destination is Pisa, where the famous Leaning Tower captures the imagination of children and adults alike. The large green space around the tower is a good spot for kids to play, and the surrounding area offers several interesting buildings to explore, including the Cathedral and Baptistery. Pisa can easily be visited in a day, and from there, you can continue on to other towns in Tuscany.

If your family enjoys outdoor activities, consider spending a day or two hiking in the Apuan Alps or visiting one of Tuscany's nature reserves. The Parco delle Alpi Apuane offers scenic hiking trails that are suitable for families, with breathtaking views over the mountains and valleys. For a more relaxed outdoor experience, the Tuscan Archipelago National Park provides access to beautiful beaches and nature walks, especially on Elba Island, where you can swim in crystal-clear waters and explore coastal trails.

If you're planning a family trip during the summer, be sure to include some time near the coast. Towns like Viareggio and Forte dei Marmi have family-friendly beaches where children can play in the sand while parents relax under beach umbrellas. These seaside towns also have plenty of restaurants that cater to families, serving fresh seafood and simple, delicious pasta dishes.

For a more off-the-beaten-path experience, consider taking a trip to Val d'Orcia, a UNESCO World Heritage site known for its rolling hills, vineyards, and historic towns. The town of Pienza is especially family-friendly, with wide streets for strolling and plenty of places to try local cheese. Another nearby town, Montepulciano, is a great place to explore with older kids, as its medieval streets are full of history, and you can visit one of the many wine cellars (some even let children see how wine is made).

When planning your itinerary, it's important to leave some time for relaxation. Tuscany is a region that encourages a slower pace of life, so don't try to pack too much into each day. Plan some downtime to enjoy a gelato in a town square, take in the views from a hilltop village, or have a leisurely family meal at a trattoria.

A good family itinerary in Tuscany might look something like this:
- Days 1-2: Explore Florence (Uffizi, Accademia, Boboli Gardens, Ponte Vecchio)
- Days 3-5: Stay in an agriturismo in the Chianti region (day trips to nearby villages)
- Day 6: Visit Lucca (bike ride on the city walls, explore the old town)
- Day 7: Day trip to Pisa (Leaning Tower, Cathedral, Baptistery)

- Days 8-9: Outdoor adventure in the Apuan Alps or relaxing at a beach near Viareggio
- Days 10-11: Discover Val d'Orcia (Pienza, Montepulciano, scenic drives)

No matter how you plan it, Tuscany is a wonderful place for families. With a mix of history, nature, and relaxation, your time in this region will be filled with memories that everyone in the family can cherish.

CHAPTER 13.
PRACTICAL INFORMATION

Money matters and Currency Exchange

When planning a trip to Tuscany and Florence, managing your money efficiently is crucial for a smooth experience. The local currency in Italy is the Euro (€), which is used across most European countries. It simplifies travel between nations that use the Euro, but understanding how to manage currency exchange and set a budget for your trip to Tuscany and Florence can make a significant difference.

The Euro is the backbone of Italy's economy, and like in many countries, its value fluctuates against other currencies. For travelers coming from non-Euro countries, you will need to exchange your currency for Euros. While it's easy to obtain Euros in tourist hubs like Florence, it's worth thinking ahead to avoid excessive fees or unfavorable exchange rates.

When it comes to exchanging currency, you have a few reliable options. Banks in Tuscany and Florence typically offer the best rates, but they may have limited hours, especially in smaller towns. Exchange offices are found throughout cities, especially in Florence, but they can have high commissions or less favorable rates. ATMs are one of the most convenient and cost-effective ways to get Euros. You can withdraw directly in local currency using your debit or credit card. Keep in mind that your home bank may charge a foreign transaction fee or a withdrawal fee, so it's worth checking with your bank before you travel. In general, withdrawing larger amounts at once to minimize fees is advisable.

During a recent visit to Tuscany, I found using ATMs the most practical way to handle currency. When I arrived in Florence, I withdrew a good amount of cash to cover my first few days. However, I learned the hard way that some ATMs located in very tourist-heavy areas might charge extra fees. Sticking to well-known banks' ATMs (such as Unicredit or Intesa Sanpaolo) helped me avoid these unnecessary costs. Having a mix of cash and a reliable credit card was useful for different scenarios, especially in smaller towns where card acceptance can be limited.

When planning your budget for a trip to Tuscany and Florence, understanding average costs can help ensure you don't overspend. Accommodation ranges widely depending on your preferences. For budget travelers, expect to pay around €60 to €100 per night for a basic hotel or a stay in a local B&B. Mid-range options, such as boutique hotels or well-rated apartments, can range from €100 to €200 per night. If you're seeking a more luxurious experience, staying in a high-end hotel or a historic Tuscan villa could set you back €300 or more per night.

Food costs also vary, with a simple meal at a local trattoria costing around €10 to €15. A mid-range restaurant might charge between €20 and €40 per person for a meal with wine. If you're looking to indulge in fine dining, expect to pay upwards of €70 or more per person. Keep in mind, many restaurants in tourist areas may be more expensive, so if you wander a little off the beaten path, you'll often find better deals.

Transportation in Tuscany and Florence is relatively affordable. A one-way ticket on public transportation in Florence costs around €1.50, while a full-day pass might cost €5. Renting a car, which is a good idea if you're planning to explore the Tuscan countryside, can range from €40 to €80 per day, depending on the vehicle. Trains between cities like Florence, Pisa, and Siena are inexpensive and convenient, with tickets costing anywhere from €8 to €15 for regional routes.

When considering your budget, it's also important to factor in the time of year you plan to visit. Prices for accommodation and some attractions tend to rise in the summer months (June to August), as this is peak tourist season. Visiting during the shoulder seasons – spring (April to June) or fall (September to October) – not only means lower prices but also fewer crowds, which can make for a more enjoyable experience. In smaller towns or local favorites, you may find prices lower than in Florence's more tourist-heavy areas.

For instance, I discovered that during the high season, staying in the charming town of San Gimignano was more expensive than during my previous visit in early spring. However, I managed to save a little by choosing to dine at local favorites rather than popular tourist spots, where prices were much more reasonable, and the food felt more authentic.

Unexpected costs can also add up, so it's wise to leave some room in your budget for hidden expenses. For example, many museums and attractions in Florence charge entrance fees ranging from €8 to €20. It's also worth noting that in some places, such as certain museums or historic sites, children or students might get discounted rates. Additionally, don't forget to budget for tips in restaurants (although it's not mandatory in Italy, rounding up the bill or leaving a couple of Euros is appreciated) and any local tourist taxes, which are often charged per person, per night in hotels.

Managing your finances while traveling can feel overwhelming, but there are several tools that can help. Currency converter apps, such as XE or Revolut, are great for quickly calculating exchange rates and understanding how much you're spending. Budgeting apps like Trail Wallet or TravelSpend allow you to track your daily expenses and stick to your planned budget. Using these tools while I traveled through Tuscany helped me stay on track and avoid overspending, especially when it was easy to be tempted by all the wonderful food and souvenirs.

In summary, when traveling through Tuscany and Florence, being mindful of currency exchange options, setting a realistic budget, and keeping an eye on local pricing trends will help you make the most of your trip. Whether you're a budget traveler or looking to indulge in the best that Tuscany has to offer, a little financial planning will go a long way in ensuring an unforgettable experience.

Language and Communication

When visiting Tuscany and Florence, understanding the local language and communication can greatly enhance your experience. The primary language spoken in these regions is Italian, which serves as the national language of Italy. However, in some areas, especially closer to the northern regions like South Tyrol, German can also be encountered, although it's much less common in Tuscany itself. Italian is central to the cultural identity of the area, and knowing even a few key phrases will make your trip smoother and more enjoyable.

In Tuscany, you may notice some regional variations in the language. The Tuscan dialect has a few distinct characteristics, like the soft pronunciation of certain consonants, particularly the letter "c," which often sounds like an "h" in the local dialect. While these differences are subtle, they reflect the rich cultural history of the region. However, in Florence and other tourist-heavy spots, standard Italian is widely spoken, and English is commonly understood in most places frequented by visitors.

Learning basic greetings and polite phrases will go a long way in helping you connect with locals and navigate your way around Tuscany and Florence. For instance, "hello" is "ciao" (pronounced chao) in casual settings, or "buongiorno" (bwon-JOR-noh) for a more formal greeting. "Please" is "per favore" (pehr fah-VOH-reh), and "thank you" is "grazie" (GRAHT-tsyeh). A polite way to say "excuse me" is "mi scusi" (mee SKOO-zee), and if you need to ask for something, "posso avere...?" (POS-soh ah-VEH-reh) means "can I have...?"

When you're out exploring Tuscany and Florence, practical phrases will be incredibly useful. In restaurants, you might say "vorrei ordinare..." (vor-RAY or-dee-NAH-reh) meaning "I would like to order..." or "il conto, per favore" (eel KOHN-toh per fah-VOH-reh) for "the bill, please." If you're asking for directions, "dove si trova...?" (DOH-veh see TROH-vah) means "where is...?" and can be followed by the name of a place. In shops, "quanto costa?" (KWAHN-toh KOH-stah) means "how much does it cost?" If you ever need assistance, you can use "mi può aiutare?" (mee pwah ah-YOO-tah-reh), which translates to "can you help me?"

For travelers looking to get more familiar with Italian before arriving, there are many language learning resources available. Mobile apps like Duolingo and Babbel offer free lessons that are great for picking up the basics. Online tutorials, such as those on YouTube, can provide visual and interactive ways to practice pronunciation and conversation. Phrasebooks, like the Lonely Planet's Italian Phrasebook & Dictionary, are handy for quick reference and can be easily carried while you're on the move. These resources are specifically designed for travelers and offer practical phrases tailored to real-world situations in Tuscany and Florence.

It's also helpful to understand some of the cultural nuances when it comes to language and communication. Italians generally place importance on formality, especially when interacting with people they don't know well. For example, when addressing someone older or in a position of authority, it's polite to use "lei" (formal you) instead of "tu" (informal you). Using formal language shows respect, and being mindful of this can help you make a good impression. When greeting someone, a friendly handshake is customary, and if you develop a rapport, you might encounter the traditional Italian double cheek kiss, though this is more common among friends and family.

Body language and gestures are also important parts of communication in Italy. Italians often use their hands to emphasize what they're saying, and making eye contact during conversations is considered a sign of sincerity and attentiveness. If you're unsure how to act in a situation, simply observing how locals communicate can give you valuable insights.

Fortunately, many of the tourist hotspots in Tuscany and Florence have multilingual assistance, so you won't have to worry too much about language barriers. In major attractions, hotels, and restaurants, English-speaking staff are usually available. For example, when visiting popular landmarks like the Uffizi Gallery or the Leaning Tower of Pisa, you'll often find brochures, guided tours, and signs in English. Additionally, Florence is home to many international visitors, so even if your Italian is limited, you'll likely find someone who can assist you in English. When in doubt, asking "Parla inglese?" (PAHR-lah een-GLAY-zeh), which means "Do you speak English?" is a good starting point.

Despite the availability of English in many areas, it's always appreciated when visitors make the effort to speak Italian. Even small attempts to use the local language can go a long way in showing respect and appreciation for the culture. Whether it's saying "grazie" after a meal or using "buongiorno" when you enter a shop, these gestures are usually met with smiles and encouragement from locals.

While you can get by in Tuscany and Florence with some English, learning a few basic Italian phrases will help you engage with the local culture and make your travels more enjoyable. By using common greetings, practicing politeness, and understanding cultural etiquette, you'll find it easier to navigate everyday situations. Along with the many resources available to help you pick up Italian, making the effort to communicate in the local language will enrich your experience and leave a positive impression on those you meet.

Safety and Health

When planning a trip to the beautiful region of Tuscany and Florence, it's important to consider both safety and health to ensure a smooth and enjoyable experience. While these areas are generally safe for tourists, being prepared and informed can help you avoid any unexpected issues during your travels.

General safety in Tuscany and Florence starts with staying aware of your surroundings. Like in any major tourist destination, pickpocketing can be a concern in crowded areas such as markets, train stations, and popular attractions like the Piazza del Duomo or Ponte Vecchio in Florence. To avoid this, keep your valuables close, use bags with zippers, and try to avoid flashing expensive items. While most neighborhoods are safe, it's best to avoid wandering around unfamiliar or poorly lit areas late at night. Always trust your instincts and if something doesn't feel right, leave the area. Additionally, respecting local customs is essential to staying safe and blending in. Italians value politeness and it's important to be mindful of cultural norms, such as dressing modestly when visiting

Emergency Contacts

When traveling to Tuscany and Florence, being prepared for emergencies can make all the difference in ensuring a safe and stress-free trip. Emergency services in Italy are efficient and well-organized, and knowing how they operate will help you navigate any situation, whether you're in the bustling city of Florence or exploring the quiet countryside.

Emergency services in Tuscany and Florence include police, fire, and medical services. In urban areas like Florence, these services are readily available, but in rural areas, especially the more remote parts of Tuscany, response times may be slower due to distance. If you're in an emergency, the best course of action is to contact the appropriate service immediately and provide clear information about your location and the nature of the situation.

For general emergencies, the European emergency number 112 is the one to dial. It connects you to police, medical, or fire services. If you need the police specifically, you can dial 113. For medical emergencies, dial 118 to call an ambulance, and for fire-related emergencies, 115 will connect you to the fire department. If you're engaging in outdoor activities such as hiking or skiing, it's also good to know that mountain rescue services can be reached by dialing 112 as well.

In case of a medical emergency, it's important to know where the nearest hospital or clinic is. In Florence, the Careggi University Hospital is a major medical center that offers a wide range of services. Its address is Largo Giovanni Alessandro Brambilla 3, 50134 Florence, and the contact number is +39 055 794 111. Another option is Santa Maria Nuova Hospital, located in the historic center of Florence at

Piazza Santa Maria Nuova, 1, 50122 Florence, with the contact number +39 055 69381. In other parts of Tuscany, the Siena University Hospital is another top facility, located at Strada delle Scotte, 53100 Siena, with a contact number of +39 0577 585111.

If you ever find yourself in an emergency, here are the steps to follow: call the appropriate emergency number, remain calm, and clearly state your location and the nature of the emergency. It's helpful to know a few Italian phrases in case the operator doesn't speak English, such as "Ho bisogno di aiuto" (I need help) or "C'è un'emergenza" (There is an emergency). If language is a barrier, try to find someone nearby who can help translate. When speaking with emergency responders, give detailed information about where you are, especially in rural areas where landmarks might be more helpful than street names.

Having travel insurance that covers medical emergencies and evacuation is essential for peace of mind. Look for policies that include coverage for medical treatment, hospital stays, and emergency evacuation, especially if you plan on engaging in adventurous activities. Many insurance companies provide emergency assistance services, including 24/7 helplines that can guide you through finding a local hospital or even arranging for an airlift if necessary.

If you're planning to explore the outdoors in Tuscany, such as hiking in the Chianti hills or skiing in the Apennine mountains, it's wise to be extra cautious. Always carry a first aid kit, plenty of water, and a fully charged phone. Let someone know your itinerary before heading out, especially if you're going to remote areas. Familiarize yourself with the local terrain and weather conditions. In case of an emergency, use the 112 number for mountain rescue.

Cultural considerations are also important when seeking help in Tuscany and Florence. Italians are generally helpful and polite, so if you need assistance from a local, approach them calmly and respectfully. It's common to start conversations with a greeting, such as "Buongiorno" (Good day) or "Scusi" (Excuse me), before asking for help. A little politeness can go a long way in getting the assistance you need.

One traveler shared a story about an unexpected health emergency in Florence. After feeling unwell during a hot summer day of sightseeing, they realized they needed medical attention. By contacting their travel insurance provider, they were directed to the nearest hospital, and the experience taught them the value of carrying important numbers and having a basic understanding of Italian phrases. The incident was resolved smoothly, and it was a reminder of how vital it is to be prepared for such situations.

For additional safety, consider downloading apps like TripWhistle Global SOS, which provides a list of emergency numbers for different countries, including Italy. The app can be a lifesaver, especially if you're not sure whom to contact. Additionally, local websites such as Firenze Turismo or Tuscany's official tourism page offer updates on local health and safety information.

By being informed and prepared, you'll be ready to handle any emergencies that might arise during your time in Tuscany and Florence. This allows you to focus on enjoying all the incredible experiences this region has to offer, knowing you're well-equipped to stay safe and healthy.

Useful Websites and Apps

When traveling to Tuscany and Florence, having the right apps can make your journey smoother and more enjoyable, whether you're navigating the streets of Florence, hiking through the Tuscan hills, or exploring historic landmarks. These essential tools help you plan, book, and explore with ease, ensuring you don't miss out on anything this incredible region has to offer.

For transportation, accommodation, and general trip planning, a few key apps will be your best travel companions. Apps like Google Maps are invaluable for finding your way around Florence's winding streets or the rural roads of Tuscany. Trenitalia's app will help you navigate the extensive rail network, especially for quick trips between Florence and nearby towns like Siena or Pisa. Another useful tool is Rome2Rio, which provides transportation options for getting around by train, bus, or car.

For outdoor enthusiasts, apps like AllTrails, Gaia GPS, and ViewRanger will significantly enhance your hiking and outdoor experience in Tuscany. These apps offer detailed trail maps, elevation profiles, and weather forecasts, allowing you to plan your hikes safely. Whether you're trekking through the rolling vineyards of Chianti or exploring the Apuan Alps, AllTrails provides user-generated reviews and photos to help you choose the right path. Gaia GPS and ViewRanger are great for offline navigation, especially in areas with spotty internet access, ensuring that you stay on track even in remote countryside locations.

Finding the perfect place to stay and eat is made easy with apps like Booking.com, Airbnb, and TripAdvisor. Booking.com offers a wide range of accommodation options, from boutique hotels in Florence to charming agriturismos in rural Tuscany. Airbnb is ideal for more personalized stays, where you can immerse yourself in local culture by renting a Tuscan villa or a cozy apartment in the heart of Florence. TripAdvisor is helpful for reading reviews of both accommodations and restaurants, and you can also make dining reservations directly through the app, ensuring you get a table at that must-visit trattoria.

Communicating with locals can be a challenge if you're not fluent in Italian, but language and translation apps like Google Translate, Duolingo, and iTranslate can come to the rescue. Google Translate's camera feature allows you to point your phone at signs or menus and instantly get translations, while Duolingo is a fun way to pick up some basic Italian phrases before you arrive. For real-time conversations, iTranslate helps bridge the language gap, especially in rural areas where English may not be widely spoken.

In case of emergencies or for ensuring your safety during the trip, several apps can be invaluable. The First Aid by American Red Cross app offers quick access to medical advice in case of accidents or health issues, and the GeoSure Travel Safety app provides real-time safety ratings for neighborhoods and areas, helping you stay informed about any potential risks. TripWhistle Global SOS is another great tool for emergencies, offering a list of local emergency numbers and locations.

For history buffs and cultural explorers, apps like Dolomiti UNESCO and Dolomiti Superski provide fascinating insights into the cultural and historical aspects of the region. Though focused on the Dolomites, they highlight how useful cultural apps can be. In Florence, apps like Musement or Florence Heritage offer self-guided walking tours of historic sites, including museums, churches, and art galleries, with detailed descriptions and background information.

When traveling in Tuscany and Florence, it's important to have apps that work offline, especially if you're exploring more rural areas where Wi-Fi might not be available. Apps like Google Maps allow you to download specific areas for offline use, and both AllTrails and Gaia GPS offer offline trail maps. It's a good idea to download these maps, guides, and other essential information before you leave for your trip, ensuring you're never lost or stuck without important details.

Before you start downloading apps, here are a few practical tips to keep in mind. Make sure your device is fully charged before you head out each day, and consider carrying a portable power bank for backup. Be aware of data usage, especially if you're traveling internationally and relying on roaming. Many apps work well offline, so take advantage of those features whenever possible to save on data. Lastly, familiarize yourself with the apps before you travel so you can use them efficiently when needed.

Having these apps on hand can transform your trip to Tuscany and Florence, making it easier to navigate, stay safe, and fully experience everything this beautiful region has to offer. Whether you're hiking in the countryside or exploring the streets of Florence, you'll be well-prepared to enjoy your journey.

CONCLUSION

As you reflect on your journey to Tuscany and Florence, one thing becomes abundantly clear—this region is unlike any other. Tuscany's rolling hills and sun-kissed vineyards blend harmoniously with Florence's rich historical tapestry, creating a unique destination where natural beauty, culture, and adventure intertwine. Here, you'll find yourself wandering through ancient streets, savoring fresh pasta under the warm Italian sun, and perhaps losing track of time as you admire the serene countryside. The magic of Tuscany lies not just in the places you visit but in the experiences you have along the way, each moment offering a deeper connection to this incredible part of the world.

For me, Tuscany and Florence have always stirred a sense of wonder. I remember the first time I watched the sunrise over the Val d'Orcia, the light spilling over the hills like liquid gold. In that stillness, surrounded by nature's artistry, I felt the pulse of Tuscany—the gentle rhythm that slows you down and invites you to breathe deeper. It's this peacefulness that makes the region feel timeless. But it's not just about the serene moments; Tuscany and Florence also invite adventure. Whether you're hiking through the rugged beauty of the Apennines or marveling at the treasures of the Uffizi Gallery, the region never ceases to inspire awe. There's a spirit of discovery here that keeps calling you back, no matter how many times you visit.

One of the most rewarding aspects of traveling to Tuscany and Florence is the chance to step outside your comfort zone. This could mean hiking that seemingly daunting trail in the Apuan Alps or sampling a dish you've never heard of at a local trattoria. The reward is always worth the risk, whether it's the stunning view after a challenging climb or the unforgettable taste of wild boar ragu paired with a glass of Chianti. Engaging with the local culture, trying new activities, and embracing the unknown are what transform a trip into an adventure. Tuscany's beauty lies not only in its landscapes and art but in the way it encourages you to be a part of it, to experience life at a different pace, and to open yourself up to new possibilities.

Beyond the iconic landmarks like the Leaning Tower of Pisa or Florence's Duomo, some of the most memorable experiences can be found in Tuscany's lesser-known corners. Venture off the beaten path to discover hidden gems like the medieval hilltop town of Montefioralle or the tranquil beauty of the Crete Senesi. Visit local vineyards where the wine flows as freely as the conversation, or explore small villages where centuries-old traditions are still very much alive. It's in these quiet, unassuming places that you'll find the soul of Tuscany. These experiences offer a glimpse into the region's authentic character, providing moments that linger long after you've returned home.

As you explore Tuscany and Florence, it's important to remember the value of sustainable travel. Respecting the environment by staying on designated trails, supporting small local businesses, and engaging in responsible tourism practices ensures that this beautiful region can be enjoyed by generations to come. It's easy to fall in love with Tuscany's landscapes and culture, but it's equally important to honor them. Simple choices, like opting for eco-friendly accommodations or reducing waste, can have a lasting positive impact.

Before you set off on your adventure, a few final tips can help enhance your experience. While planning ahead is key, allow space for spontaneity—some of the best travel moments happen when you embrace the unexpected. Don't hesitate to ask locals for recommendations. Whether it's a secluded spot to watch the sunset or a family-run restaurant tucked away in a small village, these personal tips often lead to the most memorable experiences. And most importantly, take the time to savor each moment. In Tuscany and Florence, there's no need to rush—every corner has a story waiting to be discovered.

As your journey through Tuscany and Florence unfolds, I invite you to share your experiences with others. Whether through social media, travel blogs, or simply conversations with fellow travelers, your stories can inspire others to explore and appreciate the beauty of this region. There's something special about being part of a community of travelers, each person contributing their own unique perspective and enriching the collective experience.

Tuscany and Florence are more than just destinations—they are places where adventure, beauty, and history come together in perfect harmony. The region has a way of leaving a lasting mark on all who visit, offering unforgettable memories that remain long after the journey ends. Whether you're hiking through Tuscany's countryside, exploring Florence's artistic treasures, or simply enjoying a glass of wine at sunset, you're bound to fall under its spell. So go forth and embrace the adventure. Tuscany and Florence are waiting to write their story into your own, one unforgettable moment at a time.

MAP
Scan QR Code with device to view map for easy navigation

Made in United States
Troutdale, OR
03/03/2025